William Kennedy

Published By William Kennedy
Franklin, TN 37064

ISBN: 978-0-982-94374-8

Printed & Bound in U.S.A

ALSO BY WILLIAM KENNEDY

ISBN 978-0-615-18271-1

ISBN 978-0-982-94370-0

Books:

100+ Recipes that Work ISBN 978-0-615-18271-1

Recipe Cards:

Never Eat Alone ISBN 978-0-982-94370-0

AVAILABLE ON CD

100+ Recipes that Work, CD ISBN 978-0-982-94371-7

Never Eat Alone, CD ISBN 978-0-982-94371-7

ORDERING INFORMATION

visit WWW.KENNEDYCOOKBOOK.COM.

ABOUT THE AUTHOR

Born, raised and educated in Northeastern Pennsylvania, Bill Kennedy called on the memories, background and ethnic mix of friends, neighbors and college pals, as he began to compile some of the recipes in this first book. He grew up in the "Anthracite" region of Pennsylvania, referred to by locals as the "Coal Region." His undergraduate work was through Scranton University; Scranton, Pennsylvania and graduate work was through Loyola University, Baltimore, Maryland.

Following three years as a United States Marine Officer with duty in Vietnam, Captain Kennedy returned home for a brief rest before starting his civilian career.

Over the last forty years, Mr. Kennedy has held positions as a Secondary school English teacher, Baltimore County, Maryland, an IBM Sales and Marketing Manager, Harrisburg, Pennsylvania, and business executive positions as a senior Market Planning and Strategy Analyst is Boca Raton, Florida and Atlanta, Georgia. After retiring from IBM, his business career took a different path through the woods so to speak. He became the National Sales Manager for a North Carolina based Manufacturing Company. After five years, and tremendous traveling through most of the lower 48 states, again, he changed careers by returning to the high-tech world as the Chief Sales Officer for an Atlanta-based Telecommunications Audit and Services Company. Again, five years quickly passed and it was off to a new adventure. A move to Franklin, Tennessee and the start of his second retirement allowed him the time to pursue his life-long interest and hobby – cooking.

Today, he spends his time going over hundreds of recipes and partial recipes as well as experimenting with new ones. Some of his recipes are in this cookbook. This is the follow up to the first book. If the book is successful, there will be another.

In his spare time, Mr. Kennedy is a substitute teacher in the middle and high schools of Williamson County. He and his wife Dorothy live in Franklin, Tennessee. They have 2 married sons and several grandchildren—so far. Both sons use some of his recipes and found it fairly easy to learn to cook – as well as enjoyable.

Hopefully, my recipes can help you find fun and relaxation and perhaps a hobby. As a suggestion, cook with friends and never eat alone!

Bill Kennedy

To rise at six, to dine at ten,
To sup at six, to sleep at ten,
Makes a man live for ten times ten.

-Victor Hugo (1802-1883)
an inscription over the door to his study

MY LIBRARY

The Elements of Cooking by Michael Ruhlman
On Food and Cooking (The Science and Lore of the Kitchen) by Harold McGee
Cook's Illustrated Magazine
Cook's Country Magazine
Cuisine at home magazine
Chefs catalog from chefscatalog.com
Williams-Sonoma catalog
www.cybercucina.com website for products
www.ablekitchen.com website for equipment
Barefoot Contessa "How Easy is that?" By Ina Garten
The Art of Preserving by Lisa Atwood, Rebecca Courchesne and Rick Field
The Tomato Cookbook published by Publications International, Ltd.
Encore with Claudine by Jacques Pepin
Glorious Italian cooking by Nick Stellino
Every day's a party by Emeril Lagasse
Of Tide and Thyme by the Junior league of Annapolis, Inc.
Food and Wine annual Cookbook
Joy of Cooking by Irma Rombauer (5/1/85)
Nana's Holiday Recipes by Mary Kennedy, (my Mom)
Recipes from the Coal Cracker Region of Penna.
Recipes from Jeff and Dolly Kreiger of Cape Coral, Florida

Tips, techniques, recipes and help can come from many happy folks. I have never met a sad cook. Have you?

My recipes and my books hope to continue what is very present in the works mentioned above.

There is room for more happy cooks everywhere. Try my recipes and make them your own and go from there to enjoy making something for someone – a real pleasure!

Bill Kennedy

GETTING STARTED

ABOUT MY RECIPES:

The recipes use a simple format. It is the same for all of them. The format is as follows:

1. Ingredients
2. Preparation
3. Presentation
4. Notes

INGREDIENTS:

The ingredients used in making the dish can be adjusted. You can use less of an item or more. In some cases, you can substitute for an item. Perhaps, you do not like the recipe item or perhaps it is not available in a store or pantry. Usually, substitution should be limited to a seasoning type item or perhaps a vegetable with which you have a disagreement. Please, do not substitute Fish for "white Meat" or Pasta.

PREPARATION:

I follow what I have written in the recipe. Sometimes, I adjust or change the order. It is usually based on how my helpers are doing. The main dish is mine to prepare. I let my helpers have a glass of white wine while they help, provided they can avoid hurting themselves, others, or the meal. Talk time with friends is priceless when you stop to think about it. A good time is had by all; a better time by all who help.

PRESENTATION:

I make some suggestions as to what I try to do. You can use or change them. I think it is a good idea to ask someone special for a suggestion. In the final analysis, presentation is powerful. Have your camera ready to take pictures of the setting, the guests as well as the informal preparation activities.

NOTES:

Finally, there is a "Notes" section at the bottom of each recipe. Make your changes in this area. You may want to change the cooking temperatures and times. All stoves, ovens and even the evil microwaves differ. You may want to adjust quantities or substitutions, etc. This can enhance using the recipe again. It may also lead to a new recipe for you as your "hobby" grows.

Final Final thought: *Don't Forget the Flowers or the Music*

TABLE OF CONTENTS

RED MEAT

TABLE OF CONTENTS

WHITE MEAT

FISH

PASTAS

VEGETABLES

SANDWICHES

BREAKFAST

DESSERTS

KITCHEN TIPS

IN YOUR PANTRY OR STORAGE CLOSET:

- Keep a Fire extinguisher nearby and test it annually
- Keep a First Aid Kit in the Pantry
- Store all Liquor and wines in the Pantry – not the Kitchen
- When buying food products, try to get at least a 6 month sell by date on them for storage
- Always buy a minimum 3 of each product; one for immediate use and one for later use and remember to reorder after you use the second product
- Keep a step ladder
- Keep Aprons, towels, trash can liners
- Avoid storing any cleaning products or chemicals

IN YOUR KITCHEN:

- First, read and make available all ingredients necessary for what you will make
- Keep a recipe stand on your counter with the recipe on it
- Do not begin to cook anything until all PREP work is done:
- "Mise en place" literally means to put in place (a Kitchen readiness term)
- Gather all your equipment, ingredients and food in one place
- There is nothing more frustrating than finding out while you are in process that an ingredient or something is not available to you.
- Clean as you go – do not wait until all cooking, etc. is done as you will be too tired and perhaps moody

IN YOUR REFRIGERATOR AND FREEZER:

- Label clearly all products and date stored
- Remember my 6 month rule: use it or lose it
- In business parlance, there are 3 kinds of inventories

FIFO – first in first out

LIFO – last in first out

FISH – First in STILL Here

Keep it simple: use FIFO almost always;

LIFO when needed;

AVOID FISH!

KITCHEN BASICS

Every one has their own way to equip the kitchen environment in which they work. Doing it your way should bring peace and harmony. Listed here is my way. It helps me to organize and efficiently perform. It is subject to enhancement and change but not elimination. Perhaps, there may be something listed you can put to use.

2 sets of nested glass bowls ranging in size from 2-inch diameters to 12-inch diameters: 1 oz. to 3.5 qts.
6 wood spoons
2 slated wood spoons
3 ladles, metal
1 set of nested stainless steel mixing bowls
2 wood salad bowls with knife and spoon for each
8 plastic squeeze bottles for different oil and sauces and Aioli.
6 paring knives
2 pair of sharp shears
1 set of narrow spice spoons that fit in small spice containers
1 egg slicer that also slices strawberries
2 Fish spatulas
1 lemon/lime juicer
Nest of 3 colanders
2 long handle colander strainers
1 scale, digital
1 Timer, digital
3 thermometers
1 step ladder
1 box grater
1 garlic press
1 potato ricer
WUSTHHOF KNIVES: 1 chef 6-in.; 1 chef 7-in. 1 fish fillet knife; 1 bread knife
WUSTHOF KNIVES: 3 butcher or meat carving knifes; 1 mallet; 1 steel for sharpening
1 stainless steel Mandoline
1 mortar & Pestle
1 salad spinner
1 stainless steel skimmer
3 stainless steel tongs
1 stainless steel Asparagus pot
1 All-Clad stainless steel roasting pan with rack
2 stainless steel stock/ pasta pots with lids
1 stainless steel broiler pan
1 stainless steel lasagna pan
6 stainless steel sheet pans
1 double boiler
4 stainless steel trivets
3 sets of porcelain ramekins (6 to a set) small, medium and large
1 tea kettle
1 meatloaf pan
1 food processor
1 blender
1 coffee grinder for spices; 1 coffee grinder for coffee beans
3 glass measuring cups for liquids
1 toaster or toaster oven
2 coffee makers
1 pepper grinder or mill
1 waffle maker
1 micro plane zester/grater
3 nonslip cutting boards
3 baking tray liners or Sil-pads or silicon pads
1 electric knife
1 knife sharpener
1 immersion blender
1 hand mixer
1 Tilt-Head Artisan stand mixer by KitchenAid
1 stainless steel strainer set
3 vegetable peelers, vertical; 3 vegetable peelers, horizontal
4 Serving bowls; glass or ceramic, decorative
2 can openers
Refrigerator/Freezer containers with lids for storing leftovers
2 Sets of kitchen towels (4 to a set)
2 sets of dish cloths (4 to a set)
6 pot holders
1 paper towel holder
1 hand soap dispenser and 2 sink scrub brushes
3 Le Creuset French Ovens: 5.5 qt; 7.25 qt; 1 large brazier
1 All-Clad stainless steel 14-in. fry pan with lid
2 smaller stainless steel fry pans (10-in. and 12-inch)
1 medium Saucier
2 All-clad pots with lids: 2 qt; 4 qt.
1 melon baler
1 kitchen trash can and liners (13 gal.)
A WALL MOUNTED FIRE EXTINGUISHER
A FIRST AID KIT WITHIN EASY REACH
Several Aprons—bib type

MY PANTRY

BEANS AND GRAINS

Fresh coffee beans, regular and decaf
Jar of Espresso granules
Quinoa
Farro
Mediterranean Couscous
Rice: long and short grain; white and brown
Black Beans
Kidney Beans (dark red)
Lentils, Green
Black-eyed Peas
Split-Peas

SUGARS AND SWEETS

Box of unsweetened chocolate
Box of semi-sweet chocolate
Box of Light brown sugar and dark brown sugar
Box of Powdered sugar
Vanilla Extract
Pure Vanilla Extract
Lemon extract
Granulated Sugar, coarse and fine
Blue Agave

HERBS AND SPICES

Basil, Oregano, Italian Seasoning, Sage, Rosemary, Thyme
Onion Salt, Garlic Salt Vege-Sal, Lemon pepper
Sweet Paprika, Hot Paprika, Spanish Paprika, Mexican Paprika and Hungarian Paprika
Ancho Chili, Chili Powder, Chipotle Chili, Red Pepper flakes
Cumin, Coriander, Turmeric, Wasabi, Sesame Seeds light and dark
Parsley, Chives, cilantro, Emeril's rustic, original and southwest seasoning
Herbs de Provence, Tarragon, Chervil
Spanish Saffron
Mexican Herbs and Seasonings
Creole Seasoning and Cajun Seasoning

NOTE: where I can, I use seeds and grind them to powders. Also, I have an herb garden for Thyme, Parsley, Basil and Rosemary

OILS AND VINEGARS AND SAUCES

Grape seed Oil
Canola Oil
Vegetable Oil
Olive Oil
Extra Virgin Olive Oil
Hot Chili Oil
Hoisin Sauce
Tabasco Sauce
White Vinegar
Apple Cider Vinegar
Sherry Vinegar
Champagne Vinegar
Aged Balsamic Vinegar
White Balsamic Vinegar
White wine Vinegar

- Rice Wine Vinegar
- Rice Vinegar
- Rice Wine, Mirin

Red Wine Vinegar
Light Soy Sauce
Worcestershire Sauce
Sesame oil, light
Sesame oil, dark

PEPPERS AND OLIVES AND TOMATOES

Roasted red peppers, sliced
Roasted red peppers, whole
Jalapeno peppers, sliced
Pimentos, sliced
Pimentos, diced
Cherry peppers, whole
Chipotle peppers, in adobo sauce
Pepperoncini, whole
Spanish Olives, whole

Spanish Olives, stuffed with pimento
Black Olives, whole
Black Olives, sliced
Kalamata Olives, pitted
Tomatoes in cans: whole with basil, crushed, diced, paste, sauce and juice
Sun dried tomatoes in oil

DRIED PRODUCTS

Pasta (2 boxes of each of your favorites)
Dried Fruits: cranberries, cherries, apricots, plums, figs
Dried peppers; Ancho chilies, red, mild chilies, Mexican chilies, Thai Bird chilies
Soups; Box of onion soup mix, cream of chicken soup mix
Panko Bread crumbs, plain; Italian bread crumbs
Box of Golden RAISINS
Box of RAISINS
Wasabi powder, dry mustard, Old Bay Seasoning

BROTHS AND STOCKS

Low sodium chicken broth and/or stock
Low sodium beef broth and/or stock
Low sodium vegetable broth and/or stock
Bouillon cubes, chicken, beef and vegetables

CONDIMENTS

Mayonnaise
Ketchup
Mustard, French's yellow
Mustard, Dijon or Grey Poupon
Mustard, Spicy
Mustard, country ground
Mustard, Creole
Horseradish, creamy, fresh, chunky
Horseradish sauce
Peanut Butter (JIF creamy)
Pickles, sweet coin slices
Pickles, sweet, whole
Pickles, Kosher Dill, coins
Pickles, Kosher Dill, whole
Pickles, Kosher slices, lengthwise
Pickles, Kosher Dill, coin slices
Pure Maple Syrup
Maple Syrup
Pure Honey
Wild Honey

SALTS AND PEPPERCORNS

Kosher Salt, coarse
Kosher Salt, fine
Sea Salt, coarse
Sea Salt, fine
Black peppercorns
Red peppercorns
White peppercorns
Mélange of peppercorns

JAMS, JELLIES AND PRESERVES

Orange, Blackberry, Raspberry Red and Black, Cherry, Strawberry
Apricot, Peach, Cranberry

MISCELLANEOUS

Can of Water chestnuts, sliced
Can of crushed Pineapple
Can of Pineapple slices
Can of Coconut milk
Can of Mandarin oranges, packed in water
Can of mandarin oranges, packed in juices
Can of Red Beet slices
Sack of Red onions
Sack of White onions
Sack of Spanish onions
Vidalia (sweet) onions
Shallots
All-purpose Flour
Cornstarch
Baking Powder
Baking Soda
Can of PAM cooking spray

HORS D'OEUVRES

AVOCADO CREAM DIP

PREPARATION

- In a medium size bowl, mash the avocado and
- Add the sour cream and lime zest; then combine
- Add the lime juice and salt and
- Mix until smooth
- Taste and adjust where necessary

INGREDIENTS

One ripe Avocado, halved, pitted, and flesh removed

One 6 oz. of Sour Cream

Zest of One fresh Lime

Juice of a fresh Lime

A pinch of Kosher or Sea Salt

PRESENTATION

Serve as a dipping sauce, in a bowl

Serve as a spread on baguette slices and top with diced red onion and a slice of smoked Salmon

Serve as a warm Bruschetta with a thin slice of beef (brisket)

A chilled Riesling or a white Burgundy wine is nice

Notes:

BLACK BEAN & MANGO SALSA

PREPARATION

- Combine all ingredients in a medium size: bowl
- Cover with plastic wrap, let sit. 30 minutes before serving

Note: refrigerate and serve chilled if desired

INGREDIENTS

2 mangoes, peeled and diced

1 can black beans, drained and rinsed or 1 cup cooked black beans

3 green scallions, finely chopped

4 Serrano peppers, seeded and finely diced

1/4 cup fresh-squeezed lime juice

2 Tbsp olive oil

3 Tbsp honey

1/4 cup chopped cilantro leaves, discard stems

Kosher salt and crushed black pepper to taste

PRESENTATION

Served as a dip, warm or chilled, with Tostitos chips or as bruschetta on diagonal slices of a French baguette. Salsa can also be served as a tropical salad on a bed of romaine lettuce either as a light lunch platter or as a side salad for a tuna or salmon dish.

Notes:

CANTALOUPE & PROSCIUTTO WITH HONEY-BASIL DRESSING

PREPARATION

- Slice the prosciutto slices in half
- Using a melon baller, make melon balls; or make slices about 2-inches in length with a paring knife
- Wrap the melon ball or the melon slice in a slice of the prosciutto and spear it with a toothpick to hold the ham
- Sprinkle with salt and pepper to taste
- Place dressed melon balls on a plate

HONEY-BASIL DRESSING RECIPE:

- In a blender, place 6-8 fresh basil leaves
- Add a pinch of Kosher salt
- Add 1/4 cup champagne wine vinegar
- Start the blender on low
- Add 1/4 cup olive oil slowly
- Add 2 Tbsp of honey
- Blend until smooth
- Taste and adjust with salt and/or honey
- Add a little olive oil to thicken if necessary

INGREDIENTS

(1) Cantaloupe or honeydew melon

1/4 lb. Prosciutto, sliced thinly lengthwise

Kosher Salt and crushed black pepper

Toothpicks

PRESENTATION

Drizzle honey-melon dressing around the plate and on the dressed melon balls

Serve additional dressing as a dipping sauce

Notes:

EAST-WEST SALAD

PREPARATION

IN A LARGE MIXING BOWL:

- Mix the Beets and Oranges together
- Add the water Chestnut slices to the mix
- In a separate bowl, mix the Olive Oil, Vinegar and Mandarin Orange juice
- Pour mixture over the beets and oranges and toss
- Add the chopped mint to the salad as a topping
- Refrigerate and serve chilled or warm if you prefer

INGREDIENTS

I can of sliced Red Beets, drained - (15 oz can)

1 can of sliced water chestnuts, drained (8 oz can)

1 can of Mandarin Orange slices - drain & reserve the juice - (11 oz. Can)

2 Tbsp Extra Virgin Olive Oil

3 Tbsp Red Wine Vinegar

3 Tbsp Juice from the Mandarin Orange can

4 Mint leaves fine chopped

PRESENTATION

Place in a serving bowl. This salad goes well with Pork Roast or Chops

And a glass of Red Zinfandel (chilled)

Notes:

GOAT CHEESE AND HERBS ON RADICCHIO

PREPARATION

- Heat the olive oil in a Pot on stove top
- Chop parsley, basil, scallions and garlic
- Prepare Radicchio leaves
- Slice goat cheese coins and reserve
- Place the chopped Herbs, scallions and garlic in a Bowl
- Add the HOT olive oil to the Herbs and mix
- Spread a layer of hot olive oil and herbs on the bottom of a 9" x 13" baking dish
- ADD the goat cheese slices over the layer of Olive oil and Herbs
- Cover with plastic wrap and refrigerate for one-hour

REMOVE AND PLATE AS FOLLOWS:

- Use a Large serving Platter:
- Place the Radicchio leaves on the platter
- Place the goat cheese coins on top of the Radicchio leaves
- Drizzle remaining olive oil and herb mixture over the goat cheese and Radicchio
- Serve when ready

INGREDIENTS

1 cup of Extra Virgin Olive Oil

1/4 cup fresh flat-leaf parsley, chopped

1/4 cup fresh Basil, chopped

4 Scallions, cut into rounds, thinly

3 cloves of Garlic, chopped or minced

1 (8 oz.) package of Goat cheese, sliced into 1/2 inch "coins"

1 bulb of Radicchio, washed and core cut off then gingerly remove each shell layer and reserve

PRESENTATION

This is an easy appetizer and a likeable one

Serve it with a nice chilled Zinfandel or a chilled Fume Blanc

Notes:

GUACAMOLE DIP

PREPARATION

- In a medium bowl, place the Jalapeno and Serrano peppers after being diced
- Using a pestle or masher, crush the peppers to release their juices
- Add the olive oil and stir
- Add the tomatoes and red onions and scallions and mix
- Season with a pinch of salt and pepper
- Add the diced Avocados and mix and MASH
- Add the juice of a Lime and mix the ingredients until fairly smooth
- Add the chopped Cilantro and mix
- Season with salt and pepper and Cumin and Marjoram and mix all ingredients into a dip
- Garnish with Flat-leaf Parsley (optional)

PRESENTATION

Pour the dip into a serving bowl and add the Parsley on top

Place bowl on serving platter and place pita chips or Tostitos chips around it

INGREDIENTS

2 Haas Avocados, ripe, slice and dice

1/3 cup sliced red onion

3 green onions, scallions, thin sliced

1/4 cup Cilantro leaves, fresh, chopped

1/4 cup fresh flat-leaf Parsley, chopped for garnish

3 Jalapeno peppers, sliced, seeds removed, and fine diced

5 Serrano peppers, sliced, seeds removed and fine diced

1 fresh Lime juiced

Salt and pepper to taste

2 Roma Tomatoes, seeds removed and rough chopped but not chunky

1 Tbsp chopped or minced garlic

2 tsp Cumin

1 tsp Cayenne pepper

1 tsp Ancho Chili powder

1 tsp Marjoram, (optional)

1 Tbsp Olive Oil

Notes:

MEDITERRANEAN GOOBERS

PREPARATION

PRE-HEAT OVEN TO 400 DEGREES

- Line a 9" by 13" baking sheet with parchment paper and reserve
- Rinse and drain the chick peas
- Dry chic peas in a paper towel and reserve

IN A LARGE MIXING BOWL COMBINE:

- olive oil, paprika, cumin, cayenne, kosher salt and pepper
- Add Chick Peas and mix to combine
- Toss to coat evenly
- Transfer coated chick peas to the parchment-lined baking sheet
- Spread the chick peas out in a single layer
- Bake for 30 minutes or until golden and crispy
- NOTE: Shake the baking sheet to toss chick peas after 15 minutes in oven and continue baking until done
- Remove and place in Serving Bowl

INGREDIENTS

2 Tbsp extra virgin olive oil

1 tsp smoked paprika

1/2 tsp cayenne pepper

1 tsp ground cumin

2 large cans (20 oz.) Chick peas or Ceci beans

Kosher Salt and cracked black pepper to taste

PRESENTATION

Serve as "Tapas" or as an appetizer or just as munchies or late night snack that is fairly healthy

Goes well with Chianti or a cold beer

I saw this recipe or a similar one somewhere. I think you will like it and I hope I remembered how to make it tasty.

Notes:

MY FRIEND'S HUMMUS

PREPARATION

IN A BLENDER, PUT THE FOLLOWING:

- Ceci Beans
- Extra Virgin Olive Oil
- Juice of one lemon
- 2 cloves of Garlic
- 1 tsp Cumin
- Water
- Then, blend the ingredients only half way to puree
- Add Salt and Pepper
- Add the Dark Sesame Oil
- Blend the entire mixture until pureed
- Pour the HUMMUS in a serving Bowl
- Add chopped Parsley and stir to combine
- Spread sweet Paprika on top of Hummus
- Refrigerate or Reserve at warm temp. (your choice) until ready to serve

INGREDIENTS

2 Tbsp Extra Virgin Olive Oil

2 Cans of CECI beans (15oz. ea)

1 lemon, juiced – possibly need a second one juiced

2 Garlic Cloves

3 pinches of Kosher Salt

10 twists on the pepper mill

2 Tbsp of DARK Sesame Oil

1 tsp Cumin

2 Tbsp Sweet Paprika

Flat-leaf Parsley, chopped as a garnish

1/4 cup water

PRESENTATION

Serve with Pita crisps – wedges of pita bread, cut into triangles

Toast the Pita to crisp it

Chardonnay goes well

Notes:

PEPPADEWS WITH MARSCAPONE

PREPARATION

- Using a small butter spread knife, stuff the peppers with the marscapone.
- Cover and refrigerate until ready to serve

INGREDIENTS

16 oz. Jar of Pecante Peppadew Peppers or a container of Peppadew peppers from the deli or olive bar section of your grocery store

1 container of Marscapone cheese

Fresh Chives, small chopped

PRESENTATION

Arrange the stuffed Peppers on a decorative serving platter. Sprinkle the chives over the peppers and on the plate.

As a garnish, place several strands of Chives in a pattern over the peppers

Serve with a chilled white wine in the afternoon or a smooth cabernet in the evening

Notes:

PITA WEDGES WITH SWEET CHEESE, SOUR CREAM, AND CHIVES DIP

PREPARATION

FOR PITA WEDGES:

- Pre heat oven to 450 degrees
- Arrange Pita wedges on 2 baking sheets (12 x 18)
- Drizzle the tops of the wedges with Olive Oil
- Sprinkle the wedges with the salt and pepper
- Sprinkle the wedges with the Oregano
- Place the baking sheets in the middle of the oven
- Cook the wedges for 7 or 8 minutes until crisp

FOR DIP:

- In a medium bowl (11-inch diameter at bowl top)
- Combine the Mascarpone cheese and the Sour Cream using a hand mixer
- Add the Chives and mix
- Add the Bacon bits and mix
- Season with Salt and Pepper then taste
- Transfer to a Serving Bowl

INGREDIENTS

5 PITA Bread Rounds, halved, quartered and quartered again

3 Tbsp Extra Virgin Olive Oil

2 tsp dried Oregano leaves

1 tsp Kosher salt

1/2 tsp cracked black pepper

Note: keep extra salt and pepper for seasoning the DIP

5 strips of bacon, cooked and crisp then chopped fine

1 cup (8 oz.) mascarpone cheese, room temperature

3/4 cup Sour Cream

1/4 cup chopped fresh chives

PRESENTATION

Place the DIP bowl on a large serving platter and place the wedges around the bowl

Put excess wedges in “warming” basket

Serve immediately and provide individual small plates, a good Chianti or a warm Red Zinfandel

Notes:

SOUTHWESTERN PEPPER-DO

PREPARATION

IN A LARGE MIXING BOWL:

- Place the Mayonnaise and Cream Cheese, then mix
- Add minced garlic and chopped Tomatoes and incorporate
- Add chopped Jalapeno peppers and freshly ground black pepper and mix
- Add chopped Chives and incorporate
- Using a cookie sheet or tray, place parchment paper on the tray then:
- Place the cream cheese mixture in a cookie making bag with a straight pointed tip
- Place crackers of your choice on tray lined with parchment paper
- Place pepper rings on the crackers and squeeze mixture from the cookie bag into each pepper ring
- Cover tray with plastic wrap and Refrigerate until ready to serve
- Sprinkle lightly with chopped flat-leaf Parsley before serving

INGREDIENTS

2 Cloves of Garlic, minced

6 Sun dried Tomatoes packed in Oil, fine-chopped

2 Tbsp of Chives, chopped about 1/2 inch. In length

1 tsp fresh, cracked black peppercorns, ground

8 oz. spreadable Cream Cheese

1/2 cup Mayonnaise

2 Jalapeno peppers, seeded, fine chopped

1/4 cup of Flat leaf Parsley, fine chopped

1 jar of pepper rings, mild or sweet

PRESENTATION

Serve on a platter with:

Wine: A nice crisp Riesling or Zinfandel

Notes:

SPINACH AND CHIC PEA DIP

PREPARATION

- Cook the Spinach according to package directions
- Drain and Dry the cooked Spinach leaves
- Chop the cooked Spinach leaves into a fine chop
- Place the chopped Spinach into a large mixing bowl
- Add chic peas, peppers, chives, 1/2 the lemon juice, l/4 cup olive oil, and a pinch of salt and pepper
- Combine the ingredients and transfer to a serving dish

INGREDIENTS

I (20 OZ,J Can of Chic peas or Ceci beans

1 package of frozen Spinach, chopped, no sauce

1 Red Bell pepper, fine diced

1 Yellow Bell pepper, fine diced

Zest of one Lemon

Juice of 2 Lemons

2 Tbsp chopped, fresh Chives

1l3 cup Extra Virgin Olive Oil- infused with the Zest of one Lemon Kosher salt and cracked black pepper to taste

Pita Bread for slicing into wedges

PRESENTATION

Serve as a dip or a Salsa; Serve as a stuffing in a pita pocket; Serve warm or CHILLED; And My Favorite: Add baked Pita chips coated with olive oil, kosher salt and cracked black pepper and dry Basil leaves

Prepare the Pita chips by slicing the Pita bread into triangles, coating them with oil, S&P, and sprinkled with Basil leaves then baked at 400 degrees for 7 minutes

Chilled Chardonnay goes well with this dip

Notes:

SPINACH AND MUSHROOM CRUSTINI

PREPARATION

- Thaw spinach, squeeze water from leaves and wrap in paper towel to reserve
- Heat fry pan with olive oil
- Add Shallots to sauté in fry pan
- Add the garlic to the fry pan and continue to sauté
- Add sliced mushrooms to the fry pan with the shallots
- Add the Port or Marsala
- Add the butter
- Remove the above when done to a large mixing bowl
- Add the spinach leaves to the mixing bowl and incorporate all the ingredients
- Add the Parmesan cheese to the bowl and mix with the mushrooms and Spinach
- Slice the bread on the bias and place each slice on a baking sheet
- Ladle the spinach mix on top of each piece
- Place in heated oven at 325 degrees for 15 min. approx. or until "toasty"
- Remove and sprinkle with a little more Parmesan cheese

INGREDIENTS

12 button mushrooms, cleaned and sliced

1 pkg. of frozen spinach leaves WITHOUT SAUCE

3 large shallots, sliced thinly

1/4 to 1/2 cup of grated Parmesan cheese

1/4 cup Port or Marsala wine

2 garlic cloves, fine chopped

2 Tbsp Extra Virgin Olive Oil

1 Tbsp of unsalted butter

Salt and Pepper – a pinch if you want to

A loaf of French bread or a baguette

PRESENTATION

Serve on your favorite platter as an appetizer

Have a little chilled Burgundy or Chardonnay available

Notes:

STUFFED DATES

PREPARATION

- Using a small butter knife, stuff the dates with the cheese.

Note: you may have to use a sharp knife to slit the date lengthwise to butterfly it and then place the cheese on the date and squeeze to shape.

INGREDIENTS

1 container of Marscapone Cheese

1 container of pitted dates

PRESENTATION

Serve on a decorative or festive platter. Have napkins handy, as the dates can be sticky.

Serve with a nice white Burgundy --- chilled

Notes:

TOMATO AND SPINACH TART ON PHYLLO DOUGH

PREPARATION

- Heat oven to 400 degrees
- On a large baking pan or sheet:
- Place 4 or more sheets of Phyllo on top of each other, ONE AT A TIME
- Brush each sheet along the edges with the melted butter
- Brush the top sheet with butter and Mustard to cover the sheet
- Layer the top sheet with Baby Spinach leaves, remove stems
- Sprinkle the Parmesan cheese on the top sheet to cover
- Sprinkle the Provolone cheese on top of the Parmesan
- Layer the top sheet with tomato slices
- Sprinkle with Salt and Pepper
- Place the baking pan in the oven for 25 minutes, approx.
- Remove from oven and add the Chiffenade or Basil and the Thyme leaves
- Let the sheet REST AND COOL
- Then, cut or slice the Phyllo into serving size appetizers

INGREDIENTS

4 Sheets of Phyllo Dough to make a bed

3 Tbsp Dijon Mustard

2 cup Parmesan cheese, grated

2 cup Provolone cheese, grated

3 garden tomatoes, thick sliced

1tsp Kosher Salt and 1/2 tsp cracked Black Peppercorns

Basil leaves, rolled like a cigarette, and sliced thinly to a chiffenade

Fresh Thyme leaves with stems removed

2 Tbsp melted, unsalted butter

PRESENTATION

Red Zinfandel, chilled

Notes:

SWEET ONION BRIE IN A PUFF PASTRY SHELL

PREPARATION

- In a large fry pan
- Melt the unsalted butter over medium high heat
- Add the onion slices and sauté until brown—about 10 min.
- Season with salt and pepper while browning
- Add the water and continue cooking
- Stir often until onions turn dark golden brown—about 15 min.
- Remove from heat, let cool to room temp.
- Using Parchment paper:
- Roll out the puff pastry to form a 12-inch square
- Place the onions in the center of the pastry
- Place the Brie on top of the onions
- Beat the egg lightly and brush the edges of the pastry
- Fold pastry up and over the cheese to completely enclose the cheese in the pastry
- Press the seams together to seal the pastry
- Place the sealed pastry on a parchment lined baking sheet, seam side down
- Brush the top of each pastry with the beaten egg
- Bake in pre-heated oven at 400 degrees
- BAKE UNTIL GOLDEN BROWN – 20-25 MINUTES
- Remove from oven and let cool for 15 minutes before serving.

INGREDIENTS

3 Tbsp unsalted Butter

2 large sweet onions, thin slices

1 sheet frozen Puff Pastry, thawed

1 (5-inch) round, Brie Cheese

1 egg, lightly beaten

1/1 cup water

Kosher salt and cracked Black Pepper, a pinch

I saw this recipe on TV but I recall a friend in Atlanta making it years ago as well as making a terrific HUMMUS. I have tried to match the Hummus recipe and I call it My Friend's Hummus. It is good but it could be better. Perhaps, you can improve on it.

PRESENTATION

Serve on a platter with toasted French bread slices, trimmed carrot slices and trimmed celery slices

A nice Chablis or chilled Chardonnay helps

Consider adding tea crackers instead of the bread slices

BRUSCHETTA WITH HERB-GRILLED CHICKEN AND FRUIT PRESERVES

PREPARATION

- *Preheat oven to 350 degrees*
- *cut bread into 1/2 inch slices and place on baking sheet*
- *brush each bread slice with olive oil*
- *put bread in oven for 12 minutes*
- *remove bread. from oven and immediately nib each slice with the garlic clove*
- *Spread your· choice of jam or preserves on each slice*
- *Place a slice of Fontina cheese on top of the preserves*
- *Place a slice of herb chicken on top of the Fontina cheese slice*
- *Add 1/2 slice of prosciutto on top of the chicken*
- *Transfer each bruschetta piece to a serving platter*
- *Drizzle a little Extra Virgin Olive Oil over the prepared bruschetta*

INGREDIENTS

2 boneless, skinless chicken breasts grilled and sliced thin. Use my grilled herb chicken recipe.

1 loaf ciahatta hread, use quarter inch slices Y2 lh. Fontina cheese, thin slices

10 slices of prosciutto ham; cut slices into half-slices l cup Orange or Apricot preserves with rind pieces 1l3 cup extra virgin olive oil

3 large cloves of fresh garlic

PRESENTATION

Garnish with chopped cilantro Serve a chilled Riesling wine

Notes:

SAUCES, SOUPS & SALADS

4-BEAN SALAD

PREPARATION

- Put the above ingredients in a large Bowl and combine
- Cover with plastic wrap and Refrigerate until ready to serve

PRESENTATION

Serve on the main plates as a bed

Place entrée on top of the salad bed – if serving chicken or fish

Place Steak or Pork Chop on plate with salad on the side

The wine is your choice

INGREDIENTS

1 Can of Kidney Beans

1 Can of Navy Beans

1 Can of Pinto Beans

1 Can of Black Beans

5 Scallions or green onions, sliced on the bias

1/1 cup flat-leaf parsley, chopped

2 lemons, juiced

1/3 cup Extra Virgin Olive Oil

Salt and Pepper to taste

Notes:

BILL'S NEW ENGLAND CLAM CHOWDER

PREPARATION

- Melt butter in a large pot over medium high heat
- Add onion and sauté until translucent (about 4 min.)
- Add celery and cook for 5 minutes
- Add Flour and dust the onions and celery; stir to incorporate
- Add potatoes, half and half or cream and bay leafs
- Add broth, salt and pepper; cook 15 min. in a COVERED POT
- Adjust heat to medium-low
- Add Clam juice only (reserve clams until later) cook for 20 min.
- Add clams, stir and add a pinch of salt and pepper; Cook for 5 minutes
- Add Pimento or roasted peppers, fine chopped; cook for 3 minutes
- Taste and adjust seasoning if needed
- Serve when ready

PRESENTATION

Garnish with chopped Chives

Serve with Oyster crackers

Water with Lemon slices to drink

INGREDIENTS

1/2 stick unsalted butter

1 medium Spanish onion, fine chopped

3 celery ribs, halved lengthwise, sliced into 1/4 inch pieces

1 lb. russet potatoes, peeled and halved, then diced into 1/4 inch pieces

3 Tbsp all-purpose flour

4 cup low sodium chicken or vegetable stock, warmed on stove top

4 (6.5 oz.) cans of chopped clams in juice (preferably Snow brand)

(separate the juice from the clams and reserve the juice)

1 ½ cup of half and half cream or 1 cup heavy cream

4 Bay Leafs

2 Tbsp chopped Pimento or chopped roasted red pepper

3 Tbsp fine chopped fresh Chives

Sea salt or Kosher salt and cracked pepper to taste

1/2 cup cold water

Notes:

BECHAMEL SAUCE

PREPARATION

- In a 2 quart saucepan over medium heat: Melt butter
- Add Flour and whisk for 2 minutes or until light tan in color
- Add Milk and whisk until smooth
- Simmer and stir until thick (approximately 10 minutes)

REMOVE FROM HEAT AND:

- Add Nutmeg and 1 cup of grated cheese
- Stir until smooth
- Add in the Prosciutto and stir

INGREDIENTS

1 Quart, 1% milk

1/2 stick butter, unsalted

4 Tablespoons, all-purpose flour

2 tsp Kosher salt

1 tsp Nutmeg, fresh grated

2 tsp white pepper

1 cup Fontina or Havarti Cheese, fresh grated

Optional: add 6 slices of chopped Prosciutto

PRESENTATION

Spread over cooked Pasta of your choice

Spread over grilled chicken breasts

Serve with chilled white wine

Notes:

BEEF AND LENTIL SOUP

PREPARATION

- Place the lentils in a sauce pan with enough water to cover them and cook until tender
- Drain the lentils and put them back in the sauce pot and under lid; set aside
- In a large fry pan, cook the meat until browned; remove, drain and set aside
- Add the olive oil to a large Dutch oven and heat under med. High heat
- When oil is hot, add the onions, carrots, celery and peppers
- Sauté the vegetables until softened; about 8 minutes
- Add the meat and stir to combine with the vegetables
- Add Salt and pepper
- Add 6 cup of broth and the bullion cube
- Put the lid on the Dutch oven and cook the soup mixture covered for one hour
- Remove the lid and ADD the Lentils; stir to incorporate
- Continue to cook the soup for 20 minutes uncovered
- Taste to adjust seasoning and add if needed

INGREDIENTS

1 lb. Ground Beef or Ground Round

1 lb. Ground Chuck

2 Tbsp Extra Virgin Olive Oil

1 tsp Kosher Salt

1 tsp cracked Black Pepper

1 medium Spanish Onion, diced

2 Celery ribs, diced

3 Carrots, medium sized, diced

1 Green Bell Pepper, diced and1 Red Bell Pepper diced

1 cup dried Green Lentils

6 cup Beef Broth or stock and 1 Beef Bullion cube

PRESENTATION

Serve when ready

Garnish with chopped Flat-Parsley or Italian Parsley, chopped

Serve with warm and crusty country bread

NOTE: if used as a light meal at evening-time, try a little Chianti with your soup

Notes:

CHILLED LETTUCE WITH BLUE CHEESE AND SOUR CREAM

INGREDIENTS

1 head Iceberg Lettuce, sliced into 4 wedges, then refrigerated

1 cup Sour Cream

1/2 cup crumbled blue cheese or Gorgonzola cheese

2 Tbsp whole milk, or half n' half or heavy cream

1 Tbsp diced Pimento pieces per serving

1 Tbsp crisp bacon bits per serving

1 pinch of ground black pepper or cracked black pepper

PREPARATION

- In a large mixing bowl, pour the sour cream, blue cheese and milk and then blend or whisk to incorporate
- Add a pinch of black pepper and incorporate
- Drizzle the dressing over the lettuce wedges
- Sprinkle the pimento pieces and the bacon bits over the lettuce
- Put the remaining dressing in a serving bowl to use at the table as needed

PRESENTATION

Serve chilled when ready

As a side dish, have a bowl of halved Cherry tomatoes available

Notes:

CHIMICHURRI SAUCE

PREPARATION

- In a Food Processor:
- Add parsley leaves, Cilantro leaves, garlic, paprika, Wine vinegar, and salt and pepper: BLEND until smooth
- ADD Olive Oil Slowly while blending the above ingredients
- Check for taste when blending is done
- Add more wine vinegar or olive oil and/or salt and pepper if needed
- Reserve half of the Sauce for drizzling on Fajitas when plating or serving
- USE HALF OF THE SAUCE AS A MARINADE FOR FLANK STEAK
- Check recipe for Flank Steak with ChimiChurri Marinade

INGREDIENTS

(1) Bunch Italian Parsley leaves

(1) Bunch Cilantro leaves

1/4 cup Mint leaves

5 Cloves Garlic, rough chopped

3/4 cup Extra Virgin Olive Oil – may need more if sauce is too thick

1/2 cup Red Wine Vinegar – use Sherry Wine Vinegar if you have it

1/2 Red Onion, fine diced

1 Tbsp of HOT Hungarian Paprika

1 Tbsp of Kosher Salt – more if needed

1 Tbsp of fresh crushed ground black pepper

PRESENTATION

Serve as a sauce or topping for Flank Steak slices for Fajitas

Serve as a sauce to drizzle on Steak Bruchetta with Colby-Jack Cheese

Serve with a Dark Beer or with a nice Cabernet Sauvignon

Notes:

COUSCOUS & CHICKEN SALAD MEDITERRANEAN-STYLE

PREPARATION

- Chop and reserve the peppers, the Basil Leaves and the Parsley
- Drain the Mandarin Oranges and reserve the juices in a bowl
- Put the oranges in a separate bowl and reserve
- Cook the Chicken breast in a little Canola oil in a fry pan
- Let chicken cool; then dice and place in a bowl
- Mix the Couscous with BOILING Water in a covered Sauce pan
- Add the Canola oil to the sauce pan and cover
- Let stand for 5 minutes or until water is absorbed
- Remove the lid; Fluff the Couscous and let COOL.
- Add the remaining ingredients, except for the Honey, Parsley and Avocado; stir to mix
- Season with salt and pepper

INGREDIENTS

2 cup Couscous and 2 cup Boiling Hot water

Juice of 2 fresh limes

2 Tbsp Fresh Basil leaves, chopped

1 Tbsp Canola Oil

1 cup Mandarin Oranges, drained; reserve juices

2 cup Chicken breast, cooked and diced

1/4 cup Carrots, peeled and sliced in thin rounds

1 Avocado, diced

1 tsp Honey

2 Tbsp Italian Parsley, chopped

1 Red, Yellow and Green Bell Pepper, small size, chopped

OPTIONAL: a few dashes of your favorite Hot Sauce

PRESENTATION

Place the Couscous in a large serving Bowl

ADD a few dashes of Hot Sauce (Optional)

Add the Avocado, Honey, Orange juices and Parsley as a garnish

Serve when ready

Notes:

CUCUMBER AND ORANGES OVER BABY SPINACH LEAVES

PREPARATION

- Combine the above ingredients in a large bowl
- Cover bowl with plastic wrap and REFRIGERATE

PRESENTATION

Remove from refrigeration

Toss Salad

Place baby spinach leaves on serving plates

Ladle the salad on top of the spinach leaves

Sprinkle the salads with Sesame seeds – toasted if possible

INGREDIENTS

1 large seedless Cucumber, peeled and sliced

1 small can of Mandarin Orange slices, drained and the juice reserved

3 Tbsp of Mint leaves, chopped or shredded

3 Tbsp Sherry Vinegar

3 Tbsp Mandarin Orange juices

3 Tbsp Extra Virgin Olive Oil

Sesame seeds

1 bag of baby spinach leaves

Notes:

FRIDAY'S SOUP (ALL-IN-ONE)

PREPARATION

- First, cook and reserve the Barley
- Second, cook or poach and reserve the chicken to cool; then dice
- Using a large soup pot or Dutch Oven:
- Warm the vegetable oil on med. High heat
- Add the onion, celery, carrots, peppers, and garlic
- Add a pinch of salt and pepper and sauté until soft
- Add the chicken broth and bouillon cube and bring to a boil
- Add the chicken breasts and stir in red pepper flakes
- Continue to cook for 10 minutes
- Add the Linguini Noodles and the water bring to a boil
- Reduce to simmer and add the corn kernels
- Cook for 4 minutes then taste and adjust seasoning
- Remove and Serve

PRESENTATION

Garnish with Parsley or Italian Seasoning

Serve with crusty and toasted baguette slices

INGREDIENTS

3 Tbsp Vegetable Oil

1 cup Instant Barley (use directions on the box)

4 cup chicken broth—low sodium

2 glasses (8 oz) water

3 carrots, peeled and coined into thin rounds

3 celery stalks, cleaned, sliced into thin rounds

1 large yellow onion, diced

1 Red Bell Pepper and 1 Green Bell Pepper diced

2 cloves of Garlic, minced

1 chicken bouillon cube

3 chicken breasts cooked or poached and then diced

1 cup corn kernels

1/2 lb Linguini noodles, broken into 3rds.

1 tsp kosher salt and 1 tsp cracked black pepper

1/2 tsp red pepper flakes

1/2 cup fresh Italian Parsley, chopped and used to garnish

Notes:

FRESH VEGETABLE SALAD

INGREDIENTS

1/2 medium red onion, sliced thinly

2 Zucchini or Cucumbers, sliced lengthwise in half and then sliced in thirds and then l-inch diced

1/2 cup of frozen com kernels

l can of Garbanzo beans, drained (15 oz. Can)

1 stalk of Romaine lettuce., ribbon cut

PREPARATION

- In a large mixing bowl, add the above ingredients and toss
- Then Add the Champagne-Lemon Vinaigrette (recipe follows)
- Toss the salad

PRESENTATION

Place Salad in large Serving Bowl

Add the Zest of a Lemon

Add Parmesean Cheese in chunks, small ones or in a "shavings" form

SALAD DRESSING FOR VEGETABLE SALAD

- Combine the following:
- 1/4 cup Extra Virgin Olive Oil and 2 Tbsp of Champagne Wine Vinegar or White wine Vinegar and 2 Tablespoons of fresh squeezed lemon juice
- Add a pinch of kosher salt and cracked pepper
- Whisk the above
- Taste to adjust and Pour over the salad to serve

Notes:

GARDEN TOMATO AND HERB SALAD
MARINATED & SERVED WITH FRESH BABY SPINACH

PREPARATION

IN A LARGE MIXING BOWL:

- Combine all the ingredients, EXCEPT the tomatoes
- Whisk them well and taste to adjust
- Place the tomato wedges in a very large (2 gallon) freezer bag with a zip lock tab closing
- Pour the marinade ingredients over the tomato wedges and seal the bag closed
- Turn the bag over several times to coat the tomatoes.
- LEAVE THE TOMATOES IN THE BAG TO MARINATE FOR 2 TO 3 HOURS AT ROOM TEMPERATURE
- TURN THE BAG OVER EVERY HALF HOUR UNTIL READY TO USE.

INGREDIENTS

5 large fresh garden tomatoes, halved and then quartered and then halved again

4 Scallions (green onions), slipped thinly on the bias

3/4 cup Red wine vinegar

3/4 cup Vegetable Oil

1/2 red Onion, fine diced

1 tsp Fennel seeds

1 tsp dried Thyme leaves

1 tsp ground black pepper

1 ½ tsp vege-sal or seasoned salt (perhaps Lowry's)

1 ½ tsp garlic salt

2Tbsp granulated sugar

1/4 cup fresh flat-leaf parsley, chopped

PRESENTATION

Pour the marinade and the tomatoes into a large serving bowl

Place a bed of baby spinach leaves on each Salad plate

Ladle some of the Marinade and Tomatoes over each Spinach bed

This Salad goes well with baked Salmon and a Glass of Red Zinfandel (chilled)

The salad goes well with red meat dishes also. It can be refrigerated for up to a week and still remain good.

Notes:

GRILLED CHICKEN SALAD WITH ROASTED ROMAINE

PREPARATION

- Prepare the chicken and marinate for 1 hour before grilling
- Prepare the corn and let soak in water for 15 min. before grilling

WHEN READY TO COOK:

- Grill the chicken about five minutes per side, then remove and let rest
- Cook the corn five min. per side; turn the corn 1/4 turns every five min.
- Remove the corn and let cool then, remove kernels from the stalks
- Cook the Zucchini flesh side down until the pieces get grill marks, then remove and rest; when cool, slice into one-inch pieces
- Roast Romaine leaves for several min. to get grill marks then chop them and add to bowl

IN A LARGE BOWL:

- Place the tomato slices, the Avocado pieces and mix together
- Add the Zucchini pieces and the corn and mix all together
- Chop or dice the chicken and add to the vegetable bowl then
- Drizzle the Salad Dressing over the bowl and combine ingredients

INGREDIENTS

3 fresh, ripe Garden Tomatoes, halved, then quartered

1 fresh, ripe HAAS Avocado, halve, score and then remove the flesh

1 bag fresh Baby Spinach leaves, rinsed and dried

1 stalk of fresh Romaine lettuce leaves, separated

2 chicken breasts, cleaned then grilled using my Grilled chicken and Herb recipe in my book

2 Zucchini, cut lengthwise for grilling

2 ears of corn, in the husks, place in water for 15 min. before grilling

RECIPE FOR SALAD DRESSING;

2 LEMONS, JUICED, 1/3 cup Extra Virgin Olive Oil, A pinch of Salt and Pepper

2 Tbsp Blue Agave sweetener

- Combine with a whisk and serve

PRESENTATION

Place baby spinach leaves on the serving plate and add the salad on top. Save some of the dressing to serve as needed.

HOT AND SPICY BLACK-EYED PEA SALAD

PREPARATION

- Combine the peas with crumbled bacon
- Add 3 tablespoons bacon grease and mix
- Add the remaining ingredients in order listed above; mixing after each ingredient is added
- Cover and refrigerate overnight or at least several hours before serving

PRESENTATION

Remove from refrigerator and toss carefully to combine all ingredients. In a large, tall bowl, place romaine lettuce leaves so that the bottom of each leaf meets in the center of the bowl. Place the tossed salad into the bowl and adjust the lettuce leaves so that they touch but are not overlapping. The ends should be upright.

INGREDIENTS

5 cups or 2 cans of cooked, drained and dried black-eyed peas

6 bacon slices, cooked crispy and crumbled; save the bacon grease

1/2 cup extra virgin olive oil

1/2 cup red wine vinegar plus 3 tsp additional

1/2 cup red onion, chopped fine

1/2 cup red bell pepper, chopped fine

1/4 cup (more if you want) scallions, chopped fine

1/4 cup (less if you want) jalapeno peppers, chopped fine

2 tsp garlic, minced

2 tsp dry southwest seasoning (mix 1 tsp (each: cumin,cayenne pepper, garlic powder, oregano, thyme, salt and pepper)

1 tsp kosher salt

2 tsp crushed black pepper

5 romaine lettuce leaves

Notes:

SPICY TOMATO SOUP

PREPARATION

- Use a Dutch oven or a large soup pot
- Warm the olive oil over medium-high heat
- Add the carrots, onion, celery and garlic (and bell pepper)
- Sauté until soft – 3 to 4 minutes
- Add the Marinara sauce, chicken broth, beans, red pepper flakes, pasta, salt and pepper
- Bring to a Simmer
- Simmer for 15 minutes
- Taste and adjust if needed
- Stir and cook for 5 more minutes

PRESENTATION

Serve in bowls with crusted and warm garlic bread slices

INGREDIENTS

3 Tbsp Extra Virgin Olive Oil

2 carrots, peeled and chopped thinly

2 celery stalks, small diced

1 green bell pepper, diced (OPTIONAL)

1 small yellow or Spanish onion, chopped

1 large clove garlic, minced

1 (26 oz.) jar marinara sauce store bought or home made

2 (14 oz.) can of chicken broth, low sodium

1 (15 oz.) can cannellini beans, drained and rinsed

1/2 tsp red pepper flakes

1/2 cup Ditalini Pasta

1/2 tsp Kosher Salt

1/2 tsp cracked black pepper

Notes:

MANGO AND CRAB SALAD WITH ORANGE AND LIME VINEGARETTE

PREPARATION

- DRESSING: In a mixing bowl, place the orange segments, orange juice, lime juice, olive oil, champagne vinegar, salt and pepper, then, THEN WHISK and RESERVE
- SALAD: In a large mixing bowl put the Mangoes, scallions, crab meat and mix together
- Add the Avocados and gently incorporate into the mango-crab mix
- Pour half of the Dressing over the Salad and gently mix
- Cover the Salad and Refrigerate until ready to serve
- Reserve have of the Dressing to serve at the table

PRESENTATION

Serve with chilled, halved Cherry tomatoes

Serve with a chilled Chardonnay or a fine Riesling wine

INGREDIENTS

Zest of one orange

2 large, juicy Oranges, peeled and segment slices made

1/4 cup juice from one Orange

1 Lime juiced

1/4 cup Extra Virgin Olive Oil

1/4 cup Champagne Wine Vinegar

Kosher Salt and ground black pepper to taste

2 ripe Haas Avocados, peeled, halved, thick chopped

3 green onions (scallions) sliced on the bias

2 ripe Mangoes, peeled, sliced and diced

1/2 to 1 lb. jumbo lump crabmeat

Notes:

MONDAY'S SOUP (CHICKEN-BARLEY)

PREPARATION

- Cook the Barley, then drain, set aside with lit on pan
- In a cooking pan, warm the chicken broth
- In a pan or pot, poach the chicken breast until cooked, then cool and dice
- In a large Dutch oven or soup pot:
- Warm the canola or vegetable oil over med.-high heat
- Add the onion, carrots and celery and Sauté until soft
- Add the warm chicken broth and the bouillon cube
- Add the Barley and stir to a simmer
- Add the diced chicken breasts and glasses of water
- bring to a BOIL and then reduce to a simmer
- Season with Salt and Pepper to taste
- Remove lid from soup pot and cook for 20 minutes
- Remove and Serve in bowls

INGREDIENTS

3 Tbsp of Canola Oil or Vegetable Oil

1 cup Instant Barley (use directions on box)

4 cup Chicken Broth or Stock – low sodium

2 (6 oz.) glasses of warm water

2 carrots, peeled and thin sliced into "coins" or "rounds"

2 celery stalks, cleaned and thin sliced into rounds

1 small white onion, minced

1 chicken bouillon cube

2 boneless, skinless chicken breasts, poached and diced

1 tsp kosher salt

1 tsp cracked or ground black pepper

1 tsp dried Basil leaves (Optional)

PRESENTATION

Garnish with a sprinkle of Basil leaves

Serve with crusty and oven-toasted country bread in slices

Recipe should serve 6

Notes:

ONION SOUP WITH GUINNESS BEER AND IRISH CHEDDAR

INGREDIENTS

3 TBLSP extra-virgin olive oil

6 cloves fresh garlic, minced

6 white onions, medium in size, thinly sliced

2 TBLSP sea salt

2 TBLSP fresh Thyme leaves, chopped

1/4 cup Red Wine Vinegar

1 ½ cups of dark beer – Shiner Bock or Guinness preferred

6 cups of Beef stock

2 beef bouillon cubes

6 slices of a French Bread or a Ciabatta or a Country or Rustic Bread – one-inch thick slices

1/2 to 1 lb. Irish Cheddar Cheese – slices should be about 1/4 inch thick

PREPARATION

- In a large deep Pot, Heat olive oil over high heat
- When oil is hot, add garlic and cook for 1 minute
- Add Onion slices and season with salt
- Cook onions for 5 minutes, STIR OFTEN
- Reduce heat to low and continue cooking for 15 to 18 minutes or until the onions are golden brown in color
- Add Thyme leaves and stir to combine
- Add Red Wine Vinegar and the BEER. Stir and continue cooking until the beer is reduced by half or thereabouts
- Add the beef stock and the bouillon cubes.
- Bring to a SIMMER and cook for 15 minutes.
- PREHEAT THE BOILER ON HIGH
- Transfer the soup to individual bowls that are oven proof
- Place a slice of Bread on top of the soup or in the bottom of the bowl if you prefer
- Place a Slice or two of the Cheddar cheese on top of the bread or on top of the soup

NOTE: Bread should be toasted first

- Broil the soup until the cheese melts and starts to turn brown in color
- SERVE while very HOT

PRESENTATION

Serve with some extra pieces of toasted bread

Add a little garlic rubbing to the bread before you toast the slices

ONE-HOUR MARINARA SAUCE

PREPARATION

- In a large Pot over medium-high heat:
- Heat the Olive Oil
- Add the onion and garlic and sauté until soft – about 10 minutes
- Add the crushed red pepper flakes
- Add carrots and celery and the salt and pepper
- Sauté until all vegetables are soft—about 10 minutes
- Add the tomatoes and the bay leaf and stir the mixture
- Bring to a SIMMER and cook uncovered over low heat
- When the Sauce thickens (in about an hour) then:
- Remove and discard the bay leaf.
- Taste and season with salt and pepper if needed

Note: you can use a tsp of sugar if you need to cut the acidity. Add the sugar, and stir to combine with the sauce.

INGREDIENTS

1/3 cup Extra Virgin Olive Oil

1 medium yellow onion, fine diced

1 Celery stalk, a long one, chopped finely or a small dice

1 Carrot peeled and cut into strips and fine diced

2 Garlic cloves, fine diced or minced

A pinch of Kosher salt

2 pinches of freshly ground black pepper

1 Bay Leaf

1 (32 oz.) can , crushed Tomatoes

2 Tbsp crushed red pepper flakes

Note: this sauce can be prepared ahead of time and refrigerated until ready to use.

PRESENTATION

This sauce goes well with any Pasta

This sauce goes well over fish, chicken or Pork chops

A nice warm red wine in the winter time

Notes:

ORANGE AND FENNEL SALAD

PREPARATION

- Put Orange slices and Fennel Slices in a large bowl and TOSS

IN A SEPARATE BOWL: make the dressing

- Put olive oil, Sherry Vinegar, salt and pepper and MIX
- Add Orange Zest to the Dressing

PRESENTATION

Drizzle Dressing over Salad and Toss

Add Cranberries on TOP of Salad and Serve

Note: Keep some of the dressing in reserve to serve at table

Wine: Chilled Riesling

INGREDIENTS

1 Fennel bulb, thinly sliced

3 large Oranges, (zest of one) then peel and slice into wedges

Zest of One Orange

1 Tbsp Extra-Virgin Olive Oil

1 Tbsp Sherry Vinegar or Red Wine Vinegar

3 Tbsp Sweet Dried Cranberries

A pinch of salt and cracked black pepper

Notes:

QUINOA SALAD WITH RAISINS AND PEPPERS

PREPARATION

- In a Medium size Sauce Pan, add the Olive Oil and the package of Quinoa
- Sauté the Quinoa over medium-high heat; stir until grains are BROWN in color (about 3-4 minutes)
- Add 2 cups of boiling water and a pinch of salt and pepper
- Stir and bring to a boil
- Reduce the heat to medium-low and COVER the pan
- Simmer for 25 minutes or until the water is absorbed
- Remove from Heat; Stir and re-cover
- Let stand for 5 minutes and then Fluff gently with a fork
- Add the toasted pine nuts, RAISINS and chopped cilantro
- Gently fold to incorporate
- Place in Serving Bowl; top with chopped Parsley and Serve

INGREDIENTS

1 pkg. whole grain Quinoa (5.6 oz)

1 Tbsp Extra Virgin Olive Oil

2 cup hot boiling water

1 tsp each of Kosher salt and cracked black pepper

1 Red Bell pepper, medium size, sliced into strips

1 Yellow Bell pepper, medium size, sliced into strips

1/4 cup Cilantro, chopped

1/4 cup Italian Parsley, chopped

1/3 cup Pine Nuts, toasted

1/3 cup Golden RAISINS

PRESENTATION

Place the Quinoa in a Bowl; place bowl on a large serving platter

Place Pepper strips on the platter

Top the Quinoa with Parsley

Notes:

RIVIERA SALAD WITH FARRO

PREPARATION

- Drain the Farro that you had soaking
- Combine the Farro again, with 4 cups of fresh COLD water in a sauce pan
- Bring to a Boil
- Reduce heat to medium-low; cover, simmer until tender (about 30 min.)
- Drain and transfer to a large mixing bowl to cool
- Add tomatoes, basil leaves, olives capers and stir
- Set Salad aside and prepare the beans and asparagus as follows:
- Bring a medium size sauce pan with water and salt to a boil
- Add beans and asparagus and stir; cook for 2 minutes
- Transfer vegetables to a bowl of ice water; let cool for 2 minutes
- Drain and Add to the Salad
- Stir the salad; add the Parmesan chunks and the chopped Chives
- In a small bowl mix the vinegar, oil, mustard, black pepper and 1/2 tsp salt

PRESENTATION

Pour the vinaigrette over the Salad and Toss to combine

Serve when ready with a good chilled Chardonnay or Red Zinfandel

INGREDIENTS

10 oz. Italian pearled Farro (1 ½ cups)

**** Soak the Farro in cold water for at least 8 hours*

10 oz. fresh Green Beans, cut on bias into 2-inch pieces

10 oz. fresh Asparagus, cut on bias into 2-inch pieces

3/4 cup pitted black olives, chopped

1 Red Bell and 1 Yellow pepper, cut into thin strips

1 cup Parmesan cheese, crumbled

1 bunch of Chives, chopped small

1/4 cup Balsamic Vinegar

1/4 cup Extra Virgin Olive Oil

1 Tbsp Dijon mustard

1 tsp cracked black pepper; 1 tsp Kosher salt

1/4 cup Capers; 2 Garlic cloves, minced

1 cup Roma Tomatoes, seeded and chopped

1/2 cup fresh Basil leaves, chopped

Notes:

SALADE HOLLANDAISE WITH LEMON CREAM SALAD DRESSING

PREPARATION

PREPARE SALAD DRESSING:

- In a medium size bowl, mix the lemon juice, Dijon Mustard and Heavy Cream

DO NOT WHIP

- Add a pinch of Salt and Pepper to taste
- Add 1 tablespoon of lemon zest
- Mix and taste; adjust Salt and Pepper if needed

Dressing should be in a Syrup form NOT WHIPPED

- Cover and Refrigerate until ready to use

PREPARE SALAD

- In a Large Bowl:
- Place the ingredients listed in the above order
- Mix the ingredients
- Pour in a portion of the Lemon Cream Dressing and Toss

Note: Lightly coat the Salad in the Large Bowl

- Serve the remaining dressing at the table to allow guests to add if needed

PRESENTATION

Serve as a first course for any entrée or as a light lunch

Wine: Red or White Zinfandel for entrée

Wine chilled white wine for lunch

Serve over chilled mixed greens and fresh vegetables of your choice

INGREDIENTS

LEMON CREAM DRESSING

1 fresh lemon, zested and then juiced

2 tablespoons, Dijon Mustard

3/4 cup or half-pint, Heavy Cream

Kosher Salt and Cracked Black Pepper to taste

FOR SALAD

2 Carrots, peel, julienne, and cut in 2-inch strips

3 Celery stalks, julienne and cut in 2-inch strips

1 cup Radishes, thin sliced

3/4 cup of Olives, sliced

1/2 cup Pimento slices, diced

1 cup of fresh walnuts, chopped and toasted

1/2 cup of golden RAISINS

1 block of Gouda Cheese, cut in a small dice

1 sleeve of Romaine Lettuce, chopped

Kosher Salt and Cracked Black Pepper to taste

SUMMERTIME MARINADE FOR FISH AND CHICKEN

INGREDIENTS

1/2 cup of fresh Lemon Juice

Zest of one Lemon

2 Tbsp Dijon Mustard

1 cup of Extra Virgin Olive Oil

1tsp of Kosher Salt

1tsp of cracked black pepper

PREPARATION

- In a medium mixing bowl, place the above ingredients and combine

PRESENTATION

Pour over Salad or Fish or Chicken and serve with a Nice Chardonnay and a slice of toasted French bread or Crostini.

Notes:

SWEET ONION RELISH FOR STEAK BRUCHETTA

PREPARATION

- Slice Vidalia Onions, 3/4 inch slices, and place in a large mixing bowl
- Drizzle onion slices with Canola oil
- Add a pinch of Kosher Salt and crushed Black Pepper
- Add the poultry or "butt" rub and Toss to coat
- Grill the coated onion slices until they char and soften
- Remove onions to the same mixing bowl
- Place charred onions on flat surface and chop coarsely
- Add Scallion slices to the chopped onions and chop them again
- Return the onions to the mixing bowl
- Stir them together while adding the Serrano Chile pieces, olive oil, red wine vinegar, lime juice and salt and pepper
- Taste and adjust NOTE: if you want to sweeten the mixture, Add 2 TBSP of Honey and combine it with the relish in the bowl

INGREDIENTS

3 Vidalia onions or other sweet onions

2 Tbsp Canola or Vegetable oil

1 Tbsp of Poultry rub or "Bad Brian's Butt Rub" or any poultry rub

5 Scallions, sliced (use the white and light green parts)

2 Serrano Chiles, sliced, remove seeds then fine dice

1/4 cup extra-virgin olive oil

1/4 cup Red wine Vinegar

Juice of one Lime

Kosher Salt and Pepper (a pinch of each)

PRESENTATION

Serve as a topping for Steak Bruchetta (see recipe): Serve as follows:

Slice Baguette/French bread on bias and brush olive oil or garlic on bread slices; Toast, grill or broil to warm bread until crispy

Brush Chimichurri sauce on bread slices and place a slice of Flank Steak on bread slice (recipe for Steak Bruchetta)

Sprinkle a little Colby-Monterey Jack cheese pieces on top

Add some Onion Relish to top off the steak and Cheese

Wine: Cabernet or Merlot – might try a Chilean wine

TOMATO AND CANNELLINI BEAN SOUP

PREPARATION

- In a large Pot on medium high heat:
- Add the olive oil
- Add the onions when the oil is hot
- Add the carrots and celery as the onions get soft
- Add the red pepper flakes and stir to combine
- Add the tomatoes and the Bay Leaf, stir to combine mixture
- Add the vegetable stock and stir the mixture
- Bring to a simmer and then:
- Add the beans, salt and pepper
- Stir the mixture and cover the Pot
- Cook on low heat for 30 minutes
- Remove from heat and:
- Remove the bay leaf, then,
- Using a stick blender if you have one, PUREE the soup
- Add a dollop of Crème Fraiche and 1 tsp of lemon zest

INGREDIENTS

1 tsp of Red pepper flakes

1 stem of fresh Rosemary

1 fresh Bay Leaf

2 carrots, peeled and sliced into thin rounds

1 medium yellow onion, fine diced

4 cup low-sodium vegetable stock

1 (32 oz.) can of crushed tomatoes

1 large can of Cannellini beans

A pinch of Kosher Salt

3 pinches of cracked black pepper

2 Tbsp extra virgin olive oil

A Container of Crème Fraiche

Zest of 1 Lemon

PRESENTATION

Serve HOT with a little crostini, toasted and brushed with a fresh clove of garlic and a drizzle of olive oil

Perhaps, add a sprinkle of grated Parmesan to the crostini

A nice Italian red wine goes well.

Notes:

THURSDAY'S SOUP (VEGETABLE-PASTA)

PREPARATION

- In a large Soup Pot or Dutch oven:
- warm the vegetable oil over med.-high heat
- Add the peppers, onion, carrots and celery
- Cover and sauté until soft (about 8 min.)
- Add the chicken broth and the noodles

NOTE: BREAK THE LINGUINI INTO 3RDS THEN ADD

- Bring to a boil and cook for 10 minutes
- Add the corn kernels and the water
- Bring to a Boil and then reduce to simmer for 10 minutes
- Taste and season and stir
- Remove and Serve

INGREDIENTS

3 Tbsp Vegetable oil

1 Green Bell pepper, diced

1 Red Bell pepper diced

3 carrots, peeled and diced in rounds

3 celery stalks, cleaned and diced in rounds

1 cup frozen corn kernels (optional)

1 medium Spanish onion, chopped

4 cup chicken broth, low sodium

1/2 lb. Linguini noodles or Ditalini noodles or Pastina noodles

2 (8 oz.) glasses or water

Salt and Pepper to taste

1/2 cup fresh Italian Parsley, chopped

PRESENTATION

Garnish with Parsley

Serve with crusty, toasted whole wheat baguette slices

Recipe should serve 6 to 8

Notes:

TUESDAY'S SOUP (CHICKEN NOODLE)

PREPARATION

- First, cook the chicken and reserve to cool then dice
- Second, warm the chicken broth in a separate pot
- Third, in a large Soup Pot or Dutch Oven:
- Warm the vegetable Oil over med. High hear
- Add the Onion, carrots, celery and sauté until soft
- Add the warm chicken broth and bouillon cube
- Stir in the diced chicken breasts and add the warm water
- Bring to a Boil and Add the Linguini noodles

NOTE: break the noodles in thirds (about the size of your Fist, before adding to the soup)

- Bring to a boil again, add the salt and pepper and stir
- then reduce to a simmer and continue cooking for 15 minutes
- Remove and serve when ready

PRESENTATION

Serve with toasted baguette slices

Add the chopped Parsley to the soup as a garnish

Recipe should serve 6

INGREDIENTS

3 Tbsp Vegetable Oil

4 cup Chicken Broth—low sodium

2 (6 oz.) glasses of warm water

3 carrots, peeled, and thin sliced into rounds

3 celery stalks, cleaned and sliced into thin rounds

1 medium white onion, small diced

1 chicken bouillon cube (optional)

3 boneless skinless chicken breasts, poached and diced

1 tsp of kosher salt

1 tsp of cracked black pepper

1/2 lb. of Linguini noodles or Spinach noodles

1/4 cup fresh parsley, chopped

Notes:

WEDNESDAY'S SOUP (CHICKEN VEGETABLE WITH BARLEY)

PREPARATION

FIRST, COOK THE BARLEY AND RESERVE WITH LID ON POT

SECOND, POACH THE CHICKEN BREASTS, LET COOL, THEN DICE AND RESERVE

THIRD, IN A LARGE SOUP POT OR DUTCH OVEN:

- warm the vegetable oil over med.-high heat
- Add the peppers, onion, carrots and celery
- Cover and sauté until soft (about 8 min.)
- Add the chicken broth, bouillon cube and chicken
- Bring to a boil, then reduce to simmer and cook for 10 minutes
- Add the corn kernels, the Barley and the water
- Bring to a Boil and then reduce to simmer for 10 minutes
- Taste and season and stir
- Remove and Serve

INGREDIENTS

3 Tbsp Vegetable oil

1 cup Instant Barley – follow box directions to cook

3 chicken breasts, boneless, skinless; poach and dice

1 Green Bell pepper, diced

1 Red Bell pepper diced

3 carrots, peeled and diced in rounds

3 celery stalks, cleaned and diced in rounds

1 cup frozen corn kernels (optional)

1 medium Spanish onion, chopped

4 cup chicken broth, low sodium

1 chicken bouillon cube

2 (8 oz.) glasses or water

Salt and Pepper to taste

1/2 cup fresh Italian Parsley, chopped

PRESENTATION

Garnish with Parsley

Serve with crusty, toasted whole wheat baguette slices

Notes:

BRITISH ONION SOUP WITH CHEDDAR CHEESE AND CRUSTY COUNTRY BREAD

PREPARATION

- Slice the white and light green part of each leek, LENGTH wise
- Soak leeks in water to remove possible residue
- Chop all onions and garlic
- In a large fry pan, heat olive oil and melt butter over med. High heat
- Add onions, garlic and leeks; Sauté 4 minutes or until translucent
- In a Dutch Oven or Stock POT: Transfer all the fry pan ingredients
- Add the Sage, Salt and Pepper and Add the Bouquet Garni
- add the Chicken Stock; Stir the ingredients NOTE: make certain the stock covers the vegetables; Bring to a BOIL
- Cover the pot, reduce the heat, simmer for 45 minutes
- Slice Bread in thick pieces to fit in the bottom of your soup bowl
- Place bread on baking sheet; put in oven for 8 minutes at 400 degrees
- Remove and rub bread with garlic; drizzle olive oil on each piece
- Place the crusty bread in the bottom of the serving soup bowl
- Add the Soup to each bowl
- Place the soup and bowl on the baking sheet
- Add a thick slice of Cheese to top each soup bowl
- Place the baking sheet in the broiler on high for several minutes until the cheese melts
- Serve when ready

INGREDIENTS

2 Tbsp Extra Virgin Olive Oil

A pinch of Kosher Salt and cracked Black Pepper

1 medium yellow onion, chopped

1 red onion, chopped

1 white onion chopped

5 garlic cloves, chopped

3 leeks, sliced, and chopped

6 Sage leaves, chopped

1 Bouquet Garni: 6 sprigs of Thyme, 6 sprigs of Parsley, and 2 Bay leaves, wrapped in cheesecloth and tied with butcher's string

2 quarts of low sodium chicken stock

4 thick slices (1/4-inch ea.) English Cheddar Cheese

1 loaf of a crusty country bread

PRESENTATION

Serve immediately have extra crusty bread slices available for the "dunkers". A nice chilled white Burgundy wine hits the spot and asks for more

RED MEAT

BEEF BOURGUIGNON

PREPARATION

- Trim and cut the Beef into 2-inch cubes
- Add flour, salt and pepper (a pinch, each) to a plastic bag
- Add beef cubes to the bag and shake to cover meat and set aside
- Heat Oil in Dutch oven
- Add Bacon strips and cook over med. High for 10 min. until crisp
- Remove bacon strips and put on a paper towel to reserve
- Add Beef from plastic bag to the Dutch oven and sear the beef
- Remove beef to paper towel and set aside.
- Put carrots, onion slices and Fennel slices in the same pot
- Add a pinch of salt and pepper and cook for 15 min. or until soft
- Add Tomato paste and garlic; continue to cook for 2 min.
- Remove Dutch oven from heat; Add Cognac and light a match to the cognac to burn off the Alcohol
- Return the Dutch oven to the heat
- Stir to mix the vegetables
- Add the meat and bacon back to the pot with the vegetables
- Add a bottle of wine
- Add the beef stock; enough to almost cover the meat
- Bring to a Simmer
- Cover the Dutch oven with a tight lid
- Put the Dutch oven in the oven at 300 degrees
- Cook for 1.5 hours

INGREDIENTS

1/4 cup Canola Oil or Extra Virgin Olive Oil

2-3 lbs. chuck Roast, cubed, fat removed or a top-shoulder round roast

1/2 lb. Bacon, center cut, thick, flavored (either apple wood or maple), diced or cut into 2-inch long and 1/2-inch wide strips

Kosher Salt and cracked black pepper as needed

2 Tbsp black peppercorns or a mélange of pepper corns

1 lb. carrots, peeled, sliced on the bias about 2-inches in length

2 Yellow onions, sliced thinly

1 (1lb.) bag of frozen pearl onions, peeled and oven roasted

4 cloves of garlic, diced or chopped

1 bulb Fennel, sliced thinly

2 Tbsp Tomato paste

1 Bouquet Garni (2 Rosemary sprigs, 10 Thyme sprigs, and 2 Bay Leaves, wrapped in cheesecloth and tied with Butcher's string

1/2 cup of good Cognac

1 (750 ml) bottle red wine (Pinot Noir or a Cote du Rhone)

3 cups of Beef Broth, warmed

4 Tbsp unsalted butter, room temperature

1 lb. fresh button mushrooms, remove stems and halve the mushrooms

4 Tbsp all-purpose flour

2 Tbsp Sugar

- Remove from Oven and put on stove top at med.-high heat
- Remove lid from Dutch oven
- Combine 2 TBSP butter and 2 TBSP of all-purpose flour in a bowl
- Using a fork, mix the butter and flour until combined then add the product to the Dutch oven and stir to incorporate
- Add the frozen pearl onions and mix

IN A FRY PAN:

- Sauté mushrooms in 2 TBSP butter for 10 min. then add to the stew pot
- Bring the pot to a boil on top of the stove, lower the heat to low and simmer for 15 minutes.

PRESENTATION

As a side dish, you can try bowtie pasta, or buttered egg noodles with fresh chopped Parsley as a garnish

A crusty French bread or a Tuscan boule can be sliced, toasted in a broiler for 5 minutes or 15 minutes in the oven at 375 degrees. When ready, rub each piece with fresh garlic and spray olive oil over the bread

I have tried couscous with this and it is good; if you use it, add some sun-dried tomatoes packed in oil and chopped and some chopped mushrooms.

You may not want a wine with the meal – however, a good Burgundy goes well

Notes:

BILL'S B.B.Q. MARINADE FOR CHICKEN, PORK OR TUNA

PREPARATION

In separate mixing bowls:

- Combine all wet ingredients
- Taste and adjust
- Cover and reserve
- Combine all dry ingredients
- Cover and refrigerate for at least an hour
- Place dry ingredients in a blender
- Add SLOWLY all combined wet ingredients
- Pour mixture into a medium size mixing bowl
- Taste and Adjust if necessary

For use with Tuna Steaks:

- Dip each steak in marinade then
- coat each steak with Flour, remove excess flour
- In fry pan heat canola,vegetable, or peanut oil on high
- Sear steaks, 2 minutes per side for rare to medium- Turn steaks in fry pan once only

For use with Chicken

- Put Chicken Breasts in Plastic bag or container
- Pour in Marinade and reserve in refrigerate for 4 hours

For use with Pork Roast

- Prepare a 6 lb. Boston Butt Pork Roast as Follows:
- Put your favorite Dry Rub or Jerk Rub on the roast – coat all sides
- Put roast in large container and pour in the marinade
- Cover the container and refrigerate for at least 4 hours
- Remove and Place roast in Roasting Pan; Reserve marinade for later use
- Pre-heat oven to 250 degrees
- Place roast in oven with FAT side up
- Cover with Foil and cook for 2 hours Remove foil and Add the Marinade; cook uncovered for 3 hours: Continue cooking and basting for at least 3 more hours (total of 8 hours elapsed time) add a basting of apple cider every hour on the hour
- Add a basting of Apple juice every hour on the HALF HOUR
- After 8 hours elapsed time, check temperature of Roast – remove when temperature reaches 170-175 degrees.

INGREDIENTS

1 ½ cup Apple Cider Vinegar

1/2 cup Apple Juice

1 cup dark molasses (Steen's of Louisiana, if possible)

2 Tablespoons Chili Powder

2 Tablespoons Cayenne pepper

2 Tablespoons Hungarian Paprika

2 Tablespoons ground Oregano

2 Tablespoons of Cumin, ground

2 Tablespoon of dry mustard

2 ½ cups brown Sugar

2 tsp Red Pepper Flakes, crushed

2 Tablespoons cracked Black Pepper

1 Tablespoon Kosher Salt

HALF-TIME CHILI

PREPARATION

- Heat a large Fry Pan with 3 TBSP Canola Oil
- Add the beef and brown and reserve in a bowl
- Add the Pork and brown and reserve with the beef
- In a large Dutch oven over medium heat, cook bacon until crisp
- Add garlic, onions, all peppers, chili powder, cumin, oregano and Paprika
- Stir to combine and add a pinch of salt and pepper
- Cook until vegetables are tender, stirring frequently
- Add the browned Beef and Pork and mix with the vegetables
- Stir in the beer and add all the beans and stir again
- Add the crushed and diced tomatoes and stir
- Reduce heat to low and SIMMER for 2 hours
- Taste and adjust with salt and pepper if necessary
- Transfer to serving bowls

PRESENTATION

Add the sour cream, cheddar cheese and scallions to each serving bowl

Make lime wedges available on the side

I like a few saltine crackers with my chili and a cold Guinness

INGREDIENTS

2 Tbsp canola oil

6 garlic cloves, fine chopped

2 Spanish onions, fine chopped

1 each: Red, Yellow, Green Bell Peppers, chopped

1 Poblano Pepper, chopped

1 Jalapeno Pepper, seeds removed, fine chopped

4 Tbsp Chili powder

2 Tbsp Chipotle peppers in Adobo Sauce, chopped

2 tsp dried Oregano leaves

2 Tbsp smoked Paprika

1 tsp each of Kosher Salt and cracked Black Pepper

1 lb. each of lean ground beef and ground Pork

6 slices, thick smoked Bacon, cut in 1/2 inch pieces

1 can, beer (Dark preferred)

1 (15 oz.) can each, black beans and kidney beans, drained and rinsed

1 (24 oz.) can each, crushed tomatoes and diced tomatoes with juice

2 fresh Limes, cut in wedges for garnish

1 dollop Sour Cream per serving bowl for garnish

Shredded Cheddar and sliced scallions (3 green onions) for garnish

RED BEANS OVER RICE WITH GREEN ONION GARNISH

PREPARATION

ONE DAY BEFORE COOKING:

- Put DRIED red beans in cooking pot and add water to cover beans
- Soak beans 8-10 hours or overnight
- Drain and Reserve

ON COOKING DAY:

IN A FRY PAN:

- Cook 6 slices of Bacon (sliced in 1/2-inch pieces) until crisp
- Remove Bacon to paper towel and Reserve
- Pour 4 TBSP bacon grease into a LARGE cooking pot over medium-high Heat
- Add chopped Tasso or Ham and cook 2 minutes
- Add celery, onions, bell peppers, season with salt and pepper, cayenne and cumin, then mix
- Cook until soft, (about 5 min.) stir occasionally
- Make a Bouquet Garni: 6 sprigs of Parsley, 6 sprigs of Thyme and 3 Bay leaves, wrapped in cheesecloth and tied with butcher's string and then add to the pot
- Add Sausage and ham hocks
- Cook and stir until you brown the sausage and ham hocks (about 6 min)
- Add garlic and cook for 1 min.
- Add beans and all the stock and stir well to mix
- Add the red pepper flakes
- Bring to Boil
- Reduce heat to medium-low and SIMMER and uncovered
- Stir occasionally, until beans are tender and starting to THICKEN it takes about 2 hours

INGREDIENTS

(1) lb. DRIED red beans, rinsed and sorted to remove debris

4 Tbsp bacon grease

6 slices of Bacon, sliced in 1/2-inch pieces

1/4 cup chopped Tasso, or chopped Ham

1 lb. Ham hocks

1/2 -1 lb. smoked sausage, sliced in rounds or cut in half lengthwise

A bouquet Garni: using cheesecloth, place 6 sprigs of Thyme, 8 sprigs of Parsley and 3 bay leaves in the cheesecloth and tie with butcher's string

2 stalks of celery, chopped in rounds

1 large yellow onion, rough chopped

1 cup chopped Green pepper

1 cup chopped Red pepper

1Tsp Kosher Salt

1Tsp cracked black pepper

2 Tsp Cayenne or red pepper

4 Tbsp chopped garlic

2 Tbsp ground Cumin

1 pinch of red pepper flakes

12 cups reduced sodium chicken stock or vegetable stock

3 Scallions or green onions, sliced on the bias

NOTE: if beans become too thick and dry, add some water (about 1/3 cup at a time)

- Remove from Heat and using a wooden spoon or a heavy spoon, MASH about 1/3 of the beans against the side of the pot and then stir to mix them into the other ingredients
- Continue to cook until beans are tender and creamy, (about 20 minutes, approx.)
- Remove the Bouquet Garni
- Serve or Rice and garnish with green onions

PRESENTATION

If serving in a soup bowl:

Place hot rice in the bowl and add the red beans and sausage on top of the rice top with green onion slices

Place saltine crackers on the side with a dollop of sour cream and shredded cheddar cheese

Serve with a nice chilled beer or cola soda or water

Notes:

AUTUMN ROAST A STEW FOR FRIENDS

PREPARATION

- Prepare all vegetables and reserve
- Prepare the Rump Roast as follows:
- Remove as much fat as possible
- Cut roast into 2-inch cube pieces
- Place roast on a plate and cover the meat with a light cover of all-purpose flour

In a large stew pot on high heat:

- Add the olive oil, when heated,
- Add the onions and the garlic and cook until translucent (8 min.)
- Add the meat and stir; cook for 5 minutes uncovered
- Add the Rosemary and the Thyme; continue to cook for 3 minutes
- Add the butternut Squash and the Beef Stock
- Add the Sun dried Tomatoes and the salt and pepper
- Stir the stew and bring to a boil
- Reduce to a simmer/low heat and cover
- Cook until done – approx. 1 hour; check periodically; stir, test doneness and taste
- After 40 min. goes by, add: 1 cup of red wine ; 1/2 cup of Sherry Vinegar; 3 TBSP of Sugar

INGREDIENTS

3 Tbsp Extra Virgin Olive Oil

2 medium yellow onions, chopped

4 cloves of garlic, chopped

1 Butternut Squash, peeled, sliced, seeds removed, then cubed (2-inch pieces)

3 cups of Beef stock

2 stems of fresh Rosemary

5 stems of fresh Thyme

1 (6 or 8 oz.) jar of sun dried tomatoes in oil

Kosher salt and cracked black pepper to taste

Red wine, sugar and Sherry Vinegar

3 or 4 lb. Rump Roast

All-purpose flour

PRESENTATION

Serve with a loaf of warm Tuscan country bread and a little Red Wine

Notes:

BEEF BRISKET WITH WHIPPED POTATOES AND ASPARAGUS

PREPARATION

- PRE-HEAT OVEN TO 325 DEGREES

PART ONE:

- Trim some of the fat from the brisket
- Place the brisket on Reynolds wrap in a 9 by 13 casserole dish
- Pour the pkg. of onion soup mix on top of the brisket
- Wrap the brisket with the Reynolds wrap to seal tightly
- Place the casserole in the oven at 325 degrees for 30 minutes then
- Reduce oven temp to 300 degrees and cook for 3 hours

NOTE: for 5lb. brisket, use 2 pkgs of soup mix and cook for 4 hours

PART TWO:

- Remove brisket from oven and from the casserole dish
- Pour off the juice in the Reynolds foil into a quart jar or bowl
- When the brisket is cool, cut off all remaining fat and discard the fat
- Re-wrap the meat and place it in another casserole dish
- Cover dish, store in refrigerator overnight w/ jar of onion soup liquid.
- Next day, slice the brisket(while cold) into thin slices; form the slices into the brisket shape and place in a casserole dish
- Skim fat from soup liquid; Pour SOME OF THE LIQUID over meat
- Cover the casserole dish and place in the oven
- Reheat the brisket at 325 degrees for 30 minutes
- Remove from oven and serve

PART THREE:

- While the meat is in oven, make whipped potatoes and asparagus spears
- I recommend Idaho Russet potatoes and I use sour cream and one tablespoon of butter to whip the potatoes; Salt and pepper to taste
- For the Asparagus, I use a shallot, fine chopped, a little olive oil, a pinch of red pepper flakes

INGREDIENTS

3 to 4 lb. Brisket

1 pkg Onion Soup Mix

A 9" by 13" casserole dish

Reynolds Aluminum foil

PRESENTATION

Serve when ready;

Creamy horseradish sauce goes well with the brisket as does Red Zinfandel, chilled Strawberries and Cream for dessert

VEAL MARSALA

INGREDIENTS

1/2 - 1 pound veal scallopini

2 Tbsp all-purpose flour

2 tsp Vege-Sal (optional)

1 cup sliced mushroom caps

1/4 cup butter

1/2 cup chicken stock

1/2 cup Marsala wine

PREPARATION

Prepare mushrooms:

- Heat olive oil in frying pan over medium heat
- Add 1 tablespoon butter and mushrooms
- Add Marsala wine and cook for 2 minutes, set aside and reserve until needed for deglazing

Prepare veal:

- Mix flour and Vege-Sal together, set aside
- On a cutting board, pound veal pieces evenly on both sides, cut into 3 or 4 inch pieces
- Dredge veal through flour mixture
- In a nonstick frying pan, add butter over medium heat
- Add veal pieces and cook about 5 minutes, continuously shaking pan and turning meat to avoid burning the meat
- Remove meat and place on serving platter in 200 degree oven until needed
- Deglaze frying pan by adding chicken stock, wine, and a little more butter
- Mix in separate bowl flour mixture of 1/4 cup cold water, 1/4 cup flour then add to frying pan
- Stir to reduce
- While reducing, add mushrooms and cook for 2 minutes
- Pour sauce over veal and serve

PRESENTATION

Garnish with chopped fresh parsley. Serve with sour cream or hazelnut mashed potatoes, asparagus spears and a garden salad topped with cherry tomato halves and oil and red wine vinaigrette dressing.

Notes:

VEAL PICCATA

INGREDIENTS

1/2 - 1 pound veal scallopini

2 Tbsp all-purpose flour

2 tsp Vege-Sal

2 Tbsp capers

1/4 cup butter

1/2 cup white wine

1/4 cup fresh squeezed lemon juice

1/2 cup water

2 Tbsp dried tarragon

PREPARATION

- Mix flour and Vege-Sal together, set aside
- On a cutting board, pound veal pieces evenly on both sides, cut into 2-inch pieces
- Dredge veal through flour mixture
- In a nonstick frying pan, add butter over medium heat
- Add veal pieces and cook 5 minutes, continuously shaking pan and turning meat to avoid burning the meat
- Remove pork and place on serving platter in 200 degree oven until needed
- Deglaze frying pan by adding white wine, lemon juice, water, tarragon and capers
- Stir over medium heat an additional 5 minutes or until sauce reduces and is the consistency of a medium white sauce
- Pour sauce over veal and serve

PRESENTATION

Garnish with chopped fresh parsley, watercress and thin slices of lemon. Serve with sour cream or almond mashed potatoes and a garden salad topped with cherry tomato halves and oil and red wine vinaigrette dressing.

Notes:

STEAK AU POIVRE

PREPARATION

- Crack or crush peppercorns
- Brush Dijon mustard on all sides of the steaks
- Dip steaks in peppercorns
- Heat oil in fry pan until hot
- Cook steaks 4 to 5 minutes per side
- Add shallots, garlic, stock, cream and mustard in the order listed; add slowly while cooking steaks on first side
- After cooking, remove from heat, add 1/4 cup Grand Mariner and ignite

PRESENTATION

After flambé process, serve with sour cream mashed potatoes, flavored baby carrots and long French beans.

INGREDIENTS

4 New York strip steaks, 11/2 inch thick

Mixed peppercorns, crushed

2 ounces Grand Mariner liqueur

1/4 cup Dijon mustard

2 Tbsp vegetable oil

1 shallot, diced

2 cloves garlic, diced

1 tsp salt

1 tsp pepper

1 cup chicken stock

1/4 cup cream

Notes:

ITALIAN MEATBALLS

PREPARATION

- Mix ingredients in bowl
- Form 1/2-inch balls
- Fry until brown in olive oil

PRESENTATION

Serve with spaghetti or macaroni.

INGREDIENTS

2 pounds ground chuck, lean

1 1/2 cups Italian breadcrumbs

1/2 cup chopped parsley

3 cloves garlic, minced

2 eggs

1/4 cup water

1 cup grated Parmesan cheese

Notes:

SOUTHWESTERN CHILI

PREPARATION

USING A LARGE DUTCH OVEN OVER MEDIUM HIGH HEAT:

- Cook the bacon pieces until crisp and then add the chopped garlic and stir for one minute
- Add the peppers, onions and stir
- Add the chili powder, cumin, chipotle chili powder, oregano, smoked paprika and salt and pepper and stir to mix
- Cook these vegetables and spices until soft
- Add the beef and pork and mix with the vegetables
- Once browning of the meat occurs, add the BEER and mix
- Add the beans and stir
- Add another pinch of salt and pepper
- Add the crushed tomatoes and the diced tomatoes and stir
- If needed, add 1/2 cup of good red wine
- Stir and when it begins to bubble, turn down the heat to LOW and Simmer for 2 hours. Stirring occasionally.

PRESENTATION

Remove from the heat

Taste and adjust seasoning if needed

Cover the Dutch Oven and bring to the serving table

Serve in Bowls with a dollop of Sour Cream, shredded cheddar and Scallion slices on top

Saltine crackers or a slice of garlic rubbed Texas Toast might go well for youHave ice-cold beer to serve with your chili and a little country western music for listening

INGREDIENTS

1 lb. each or ground-round beef, ground pork and ground chuck beef

8 slices of thick-cut or center-cut applewood or smoked bacon cut into 1/2-inch pieces

2 yellow onions, rough-chopped

1 red, yellow, green and poblano pepper, each rough-chopped

5 cloves of garlic, fine chopped

3 Tbsp chili powder

1 Tbsp ground cumin

1 Tbsp chipotle chili powder

2 Tbsp smoked paprika

1 Tbsp oregano leaves

2 Tbsp red pepper flakes

1 tsp kosher salt

1 tsp cracked black pepper

1 can of your favorite beer

1 (15 oz.) can each of pinto beans, black beans, and kidney beans, drained and rinsed

1 (24-oz.) can crushed tomatoes

1 (24-oz.) can diced tomatoes and their juices

FOR A GARNISH:

Sour cream and shredded cheddar cheese

Scallions, sliced on the bias

GREEN APPLE SAUERKRAUT WITH BRATWURST

PREPARATION

- Remove sauerkraut from package, drain and dry it, set aside
- Heat 2 tablespoons of olive oil in large frying pan
- Add sweet onion slices and sauté for 3 minutes
- Add a third of the diced apples to the onions and sauté for 2 minutes
- Add 1⁄4 cup white wine
- Add half of the sauerkraut
- Add 1 teaspoon caraway seeds
- Continue to sauté and toss or mix the sauerkraut and onions for 3 minutes
- Add remaining apples
- Add remaining sauerkraut
- Add 1 teaspoon caraway seeds
- Add 1⁄4 cup white wine
- Add salt and pepper
- Continue to mix and toss for 3 minutes
- Remove from heat and pour into baking dish
- Add cumin, cayenne pepper and cinnamon
- Prepare brats separately boiling in water 5 minutes, then browning in frying pan 3 minutes
- Place cooked bratwursts on top of sauerkraut to bake
- Pour or sprinkle1/4 cup white wine, pinch of salt, pinch of pepper and 2 teaspoons caraway seeds on top of bratwursts
- Cover dish with foil and bake at 375 for 20 minutes
- Remove foil and continue to bake at 375 until brown (about 10 minutes)

INGREDIENTS

2 Tbsp olive oil

2 pounds sauerkraut (bag)

3 Granny Smith apples, peeled and diced

4 tsp caraway seeds

1 large sweet onion, sliced

Salt to taste

Pepper to taste

1 tsp cumin

1 tsp cayenne pepper

1 tsp cinnamon

6 bratwursts

3/4 cup white wine

PRESENTATION

Serve with garlic or green onion mashed potatoes. Note: this dish can be prepared with various kinds of sausages, franks, pork chops or ribs.

WHITE MEAT

BAKED CHICKEN THIGHS WITH SWEET CHILI GLAZE

PREPARATION

- Combine all ingredients for the Marinade in a large Resealable plastic hag; add the chicken thighs; seal the bag

REFRIGERATE FOR 8 HOURS OR OVERNIGHT

PREPARATION FOR COOKING:

- Remove chicken from the marinade and place each piece in a 13 by I)·inch baking dish or pan
- Reserve 1/4 cup of marinade; strain to remove all herbs, etc.
- PRE-HEAT THE OVEN TO 350 DEGREES
- BAKE THE CHICKEN THIGHS .FOR 45 MINUTES

INGREDIENTS

2 lbs. boneless, skinless Chicken thighs should serve 4

INGREDIENTS FOR MARINADE:

4 Tbsp fresh Orange Zest

1 cup fresh squeezed Orange Juice (3 Calif. Navel oranges)

1 teasp kosher salt; 2 teasp freshly cracked black pepper

chiffonade 8 Mint leaves and 10 fresh Basil leaves

1 Tbsp celery seeds

3 scallions, thinly sliced; 2 fresh shallots, fine chopped

1/4 cup white balsamic vinegar

RECIPE FOR SWEET CHILI GLAZE ON FOLLOWING PAGE

Notes:

SWEET CHILI GLAZE

PREPARATION

IN A MEDIUM SAUCE PAN OVER MEDIUM-HIGH HEAT:

- Add the extra virgin olive oil; when oil is HOT
- Add shallots and ginger and saute for 3 minutes

Add the remaining ingredients and stir

- Reduce heat to a low and simmer for 15 minutes
- Remove from heat and prepare to baste the chicken as follows
- After chicken bakes for 45 minutes:
- Remove chicken from oven, baste the tops and turn the chicken pieces over
- Baste the bottoms and return the chicken dish to the oven and continue to cook
- Baste the chicken at intervals of 8 minutes or for 24 minutes, turning and basting every eight minutes
- Remove from oven; arrange on serving platter
- Garnish with chopped Chives or Cilantro leaves
- SERVE WHEN READY

INGREDIENTS

1 Tbsp extra virgin olive oil

1 shallot, fine-chopped or minced

1 Tbsp fresh Ginger, peeled. sliced and fine·chopped

1 cup Orange marmalade with fine·chopped rinds

1/4 cup plus 2 Tbsp Sweet Chili Sauce

I t red pepper flakes

2 Tbsp white balsamic vinegar

AND ADD 1/4 CUP OF STRAINED RESERVED MARINADE

PRESENTATION

Serve with Island Rice or a nice white rice with golden RAISINS mixed in

A chilled Zinfandel is my wine of choice

Notes:

CHINESE CHICKEN WITH ORZO-PEPPER SALAD

PREPARATION

USE A SMALL BOWL TO COMBINE:

- Oil, vinegar, soy sauce and hoisin sauce
- Whisk, cover with plastic wrap and reserve

USE A LARGE BOWL AND MIX:

- Orzo, water chestnuts, chicken, onions and peppers
- Add sugar snap peas and toss
- Pour Dressing over the mixture and mix to coat
- Toast almonds and sesame seeds for garnish
- Cover with plastic wrap and Refrigerate

INGREDIENTS

1 (9oz) pkg. Sugar snap peas, frozen

1 (16oz) pkg. Orzo, cooked, drained and reserved

1 cup water chestnuts, drained and chopped

3 cup Chicken, cooked and diced

3 Scallions, chopped

I Red Bell Pepper, chopped

1 Green or Yellow Bell Pepper, chopped

1/2 cup Vegetable oil

3 Tbsp Rice Wine Vinegar

2 Tbsp Soy Sauce

2teasp Hoisin Sauce

1 (2oz) pkg. Toasted, slivered almonds

Sesame seeds, toasted for garnish

PRESENTATION

Serve chilled or at room temperature

Notes:

CHICKEN FUSILI
WITH PESTO AND CHERRY TOMATOES

PREPARATION

- In a large fry pan:
- Use med. High heat and cook the cubed chicken in Olive Oil
- In a BLENDER:
- Combine the parsley, nuts, salt and pepper and garlic cloves
- Add the 3 TBSP of Olive Oil and blend to a runny pesto state
- Cook the Pasta to an al dente state (about 8 min.)

LASTLY:

- Place hot pasta in a large bowl
- Pour Pesto over the chicken as it cooks in the fry pan
- When cooked, Pour pesto and chicken over the cooked Pasta
- Toss and then add a pinch of red pepper flakes, the cherry tomatoes and serve

INGREDIENTS

2 large skinless, boneless chicken breasts, diced or cubed cut

1/2 cup Pistachio nuts or pine nuts or almond slices

A full cup of fresh, Flat-Leaf Parsley or Italian Parsley

5 large cloves of garlic, peeled

A pinch of Kosher Salt and Cracked Black Pepper

3 Tbsp of Extra Virgin Olive Oil

1 pound of Fusili Pasta or Rotini Pasta

1 pound of Cherry tomatoes, halved

Red pepper flakes

PRESENTATION

Serve with a side bowl of grated Parmesan cheese for table use

Serve with a warmed loaf of Italian bread, sliced on bias

Chianti or a nice red table wine adds a little kick

Notes:

COUNTRY-FRIED PORK CHOPS PREPARED IN A BRINE MARINADE

PREPARATION

- Place all ingredients in the plastic bag and close it
- Place bag in refrigerator
- Let products marinate in brine for about 3 hours
- Remove and pat dry with paper towels
- Sprinkle the chops with salt and pepper
- Dredge the dried chops in a mixture of Flour
- Pat or shake off the excess flour
- Fry chops in a little vegetable oil on medium high heat
- 3-4 minutes per side depending on thickness

INGREDIENTS

1 large plastic Zip-top bag

3 cup cold water

1/4 cup kosher salt

1/4 cup granulated sugar

4 Pork chops – 1/4-1/2 inch thick, each

2 cup Ice cubes

PRESENTATION

Use a large serving platter

Arrange the chops on the platter

Pour the "Country Gravy" over the chops – see recipe for the Country Gravy

Garnish with slices of Scallion onions

Note: This goes well with Home Fried potatoes and Green String Beans and Fresh Tomato slices

Notes:

LEMON CHICKEN WITH ARTICHOKES AND ASPARAGUS

PREPARATION

- Using a large fry pan:
- Heat 2 tbsp Olive Oil
- Add chicken and cook until light golden brown
- Remove and reserve the cooked chicken
- Add onions and garlic with a tbsp of evoo and sauté until translucent
- Add artichokes and Asparagus pieces to the sauté
- Add diced chicken back to the mix and Salt and Pepper to taste
- Stir and continue to sauté adding the water and the wine
- Stir the mix add lemon zest and lemon juice
- Add the basil leaves and cover the fry pan with a lid
- Cook on low heat for 5 minutes
- Stir and Serve

INGREDIENTS

3tbsp extra virgin olive oil

1 yellow onion, diced

10 Basil leaves, rolled and sliced into ribbons

1/2 bunch of Asparagus, chopped into 2 inch pieces

1 can of Artichoke hearts, quartered, drained

3 cloves of garlic, sliced

Kosher Salt and fresh cracked Pepper to taste

4 chicken breasts, boneless, skinless and diced

1/3 cup water

1/3 cup white wine—Sauvignon Blanc or Chablis

1 tsp grated lemon zest

Fresh Italian Parsley for garnish

Sliced Italian bread warmed on a baking sheet in the oven at 300 Degrees

PRESENTATION

Place the cooked meal in a large serving bowl

Garnish with fresh Italian Parsley, chopped

Ladle the meal to each place setting and serve grated Parmesan cheese to the side with crusty slices of Italian bread

Wine could be a chilled Pinot Grigio; or a Chardonnay of your choice

Notes:

GRILLED CHICKEN SALAD WITH ROASTED ROMAINE

PREPARATION

- Prepare the chicken and marinate for 1 hour before grilling
- Prepare the com and let soak in water for 15 min. before grilling

WHEN READY TO COOK:

- Grill the chicken about five minutes per side, then remove and let rest
- Cook the corn five min. per side; turn the corn 1/4 turns every five min. Remove the com and let cool then, remove kernels from the stalks Cook the Zucchini flesh side down until the pieces get grill marks, then remove and rest; when cool, slice into one-inch pieces
- Roast Romaine leaves for several min. to get grill marks then chop them and add to bowl

IN A LARGE BOWL:

- Place the tomato slices, the Avocado pieces and mix together
- Add the Zucchini pieces and the corn and mix all together
- Chop or dice the chicken and add to the vegetable bowl then Drizzle the Salad Dressing over the bowl and combine ingredients

RECIPE FOR SALAD DRESSING

- 2 LEMONS, JUICED
- 1/3 cup Extra Virgin Olive Oil
- A pinch of Salt and Pepper
- 2 TBSP Blue Agave sweetener
- Combine with a whisk and serve

INGREDIENTS

3 fresh. ripe Garden Tomatoes, halved, then quartered

1 fresh, ripe HAAS Avocado, halve, score and then remove the flesh

1 bag fresh Baby Spinach leaves, rinsed and dried

1 stalk of fresh Romaine lettuce leaves, separated

2 chicken breasts, cleaned then grilled using my Grilled chicken and Herb recipe in my book

2 Zucchini, cut lengthwise for grilling

2 ears of corn, in the husks, place in water for 15 min. before grilling

PRESENTATION

Place baby spinach leaves on the serving plate and add the salad on top.

Save some of the dressing to serve as needed

HOT SKILLET PORK CHOPS WITH APPLES AND RAISINS

PREPARATIONS

PART ONE: PREPARE THE CHOPS

- Heat a skillet until HOT
- Add 2 tablespoons of Oil until Hot
- Salt and Pepper the filleted Pork Chops and add to the skillet
- Sauté chops for 1 minute per side then remove from skillet and wrap in foil to reserve
- IN THE SAME SKILLET (do not remove juices or clean skillet) Add:
- 1/4 cup of Apple Cider
- 1/4 cup of Apple Cider Vinegar
- Apple slices and Add back the Pork Chops
- Cook in Med. High Heat until chops are done and the apples have somewhat softened

PART TWO: PREPARE THE SAUCE

- In a separate sauce pan:
- Add the following:1/4 cup Apple Cider Vinegar
- 1/4 cup Apple Cider, 1/2 cup light Brown Sugar, 1/4 cup Orange Juice,1 Cinnamon stick, 1/4 cup Golden RAISINS, and several of the Orange Slices
- Using medium-high heat, REDUCE the Sauce by 1/2
- Then, Strain the sauce and return it to sauce pan
- Heat on Medium-LOW until further reduction and thickening occurs to your satisfaction

INGREDIENTS

4 "thick" Pork Chops, (about 2 inch thick), butterfly the chops

1/2 cup Apple Cider

1/2 cup Apple Cider Vinegar

3 Granny Smith Apples, peeled, halved, quartered and sliced thin

1/4 cup Golden RAISINS

A Pinch of Kosher Salt and a pinch of cracked Black Pepper

2 Tbsp Vegetable Oil or Canola Oil

1/2 cup Orange Juice

1/2 cup light Brown Sugar

1 Cinnamon Stick

1/2 Orange, sliced thinly with skin on

PRESENTATION

Place the Chops on a Serving Platter

Drizzle some sauce over the chops and reserve the remainder to a serving bowl Add Orange slices and Fresh Parsley as a Garnish around the Platter

Serve with a Chilled Riesling or Chardonnay Mashed Potatoes with Chives or Sweet Potatoes with Molasses flavoring as a side.

PORK LOIN ROAST WITH APRICOT, PEACH AND PLUM GLAZE

INGREDIENTS

4-pound pork loin roast, filleted and tied

1/4 cup Dijon mustard

1/4 cup brown sugar

1/4 cup orange juice

1 cup each of dried apricots, peaches and plums – slice the dried fruit in quarters

3/4 cup Port wine

1/8 t Allspice

2 Tbsp Cornstarch

PREPARATION

- Pre-heat oven to 350 degrees
- Fillet the roast or open it to lay flat;
- Use a little olive oil on the inside of the roast
- Mix Rosemary, Thyme and Sage together with a pinch of Kosher salt and crushed black pepper; spread on the inside of the roast and fold the roast together
- Using butcher's twine, tie the roast every 2-inches (about 5 pieces of string – each piece is about a shoe lace size piece)and cut the excess strings
- Combine mustard and 2 tablespoons of brown sugar and spread over the roast
- Place roast on a rack in a roasting pan and cook for one and 1/2 hours
- Meanwhile: Combine remaining brown sugar, orange juice, dried fruits, Port wine and allspice in a saucepan
- Cook the ingredients on the stove top over high heat
- Bring to a boil, reduce heat to low, cover and simmer for 15 minutes
- Spoon fruit mixture around roast DURING THE LAST 30 MINUTES of roasting time.

NOTE: Roast the meat until the internal temperature reads 155-160 degrees on a meat thermometer

- Transfer roast and fruits when done to a serving platter; remove strings; cover with Alum. Foil to keep warm
- Combine remaining orange juice and Cornstarch; gradually whisk into the roasting pan liquid and cook over medium heat, stirring until slightly thickens

PRESENTATION

Serve the roast sliced; slices could line up with where you tied the strings;

Serve the cook fruit around the roast on the platter

Serve the juices or glaze by pouring or dripping over the roast slices; reserve some in a gravy boat for serving at the table

Wine can be a chilled Red Zinfandel or a Merlot; some folks like a Reisling or a Chablis.

STOVE-TOP PORK CHOPS EUROPEAN-STYLE
WITH CARROTS AND CAPERS IN A TOMATO-FENNEL SAUCE

PREPARATION

- In a large cast iron skillet or Brasier heat the Olive Oil over high heat.
- Season the Pork chops with the salt and pepper mixture
- Add the chops to the hot pan seasoned side down; season the top side.
- Brown all sides (about 4 min. top and bottom; one min. on each side.)
- Remove the pork chops to a platter and cover with tin foil to reserve.
- Add Fennel slices, Carrots, Shallots and 1/4 cup of the Parsley to the pan
- Cook over medium heat until browning begins (about 4-5 min.)
- Add wine using a wooden spoon scrape brown bits off pan bottom.
- Add the tomatoes and the pinch of salt and pepper and stir.
- Place pork chops back in pan; keep them separated in the sauce.
- Cook until the fennel slices and carrots are tender; May take 15 to 18 minutes until ready; Remove and plate immediately

INGREDIENTS

4 (2-inch thick) boneless pork chops

4 Tbsp Extra virgin Olive Oil

2 tsp each of Kosher Salt and Cracked Black Pepper Mixed together for seasoning Chops

A pinch of Kosher Salt and Cracked Black Pepper to use while making the Sauce

2 Fennel Bulbs, cored and sliced thinly; save the fronds for use in the making of the Sauce and for Garnish

3 Shallots, sliced thinly

2 carrots, peeled and sliced on bias thinly

1 Red Bell and 1 Yellow Bell pepper, cut into strips

1/2 cup Italian flat-leaf Parsley, chopped

1/2 cup White Wine (preferably a Sauvignon Blanc)

1 can (28 oz.) diced tomatoes, plain with juices

Zest of a Lemon

3 Tbsp Capers in Brine

PRESENTATION

Place the pork chops on a serving platter.

To finish the Sauce, add the lemon zest to the mixture and stir

Add the remaining parsley and capers and stir

Taste and adjust the sauce with an additional pinch of salt and pepper if necessary

SPOON THE SAUCE OVER THE PORK CHOPS ON THE SERVING PLATTER

Red Zinfandel Wine, chilled is terrific

PORK TENDERLOIN WITH RED ONION & SPINACH ROULADE AND ROMESCO SAUCE

PREPARATION

- In a large Fry Pan:
- Sauté chopped red onion in EVOO until soft
- Add the chopped garlic and the chopped Spinach
- Add the Honey and the Sherry Vinegar and the water
- Again, add a pinch of salt and pepper
- REDUCE THE MIXTURE
- Butterfly the Pork Tenderloins
- Place plastic wrap over the meat and pound it FLAT
- Season the flattened Pork with salt and pepper
- Layer the Pork with a layer of Ham slices
- Add the Onion and Spinach mixture on top of the ham
- Layer onion and spinach mixture with a layer of Roasted red Peppers
- ROLL THE PORK AND THEN TIE IT WITH STRING
- Heat a large Fry Pan with EVOO
- Place the string-tied pork in the fry pan and sear the meat on all sides
- Place the meat in a pre-heated OVEN at 450 degrees and bake for 10-15 minutes or until meat is 140-145 degrees temperature
- Remove meat and slice it in 1-inch slices
- Plate the meat and drizzle the Romesco Sauce over the middle of the slices
- Reserve the remaining sauce to serve in a bowl at the table

INGREDIENTS

1 Medium Red Onion, diced

2Tbsp Extra virgin Olive Oil

4 Cloves Garlic, chopped

1 lb. Baby Spinach leaves, chopped roughly

3 Tbsp Honey

1/4 cup Sherry Vinegar

1/4 cup water

A pinch of Kosher salt and cracked black pepper

2 Pork Tenderloins

4 slices of Serrano Ham or Prosciutto

FOR THE ROMESCO SAUCE:

4 large slices of roasted red peppers or 1 large roasted red pepper, peeled, seeded and sliced

2 Tbsp of capers

1/2 cup seasoned bread crumbs, toasted or a large, thick slice of country bread, toasted on both sides and diced

3/4 cup Extra Virgin Olive Oil

A pinch of salt and pepper

3/4 cup Almond slices, toasted

1 tsp Cayenne pepper

3 tsp garlic, minced

1 large garden tomato, peeled, seeded and diced

1 tsp Paprika

1/4 cup Red Wine Vinegar

RECIPE FOR ROMESCO SAUCE

USING A FOOD PROCESSOR OR BLENDER:

- Put bread or bread crumbs in Food Processor
- Add the Almonds, cayenne pepper and garlic
- Pulse to combine
- Add the red pepper, tomato, paprika, salt and pepper
- Blend to form a chunky Paste
- Add red wine vinegar and PULSE once
- Add Olive Oil while the Food Processor is running
- Continue to run until mixture emulsifies
- Taste and Adjust
- Pour Sauce in a Serving bowl and reserve in a warm oven or on stove top on low heat

PRESENTATION

Mediterranean Couscous or Rice Pilaf with almonds and cranberries goes well with the Pork Roulade

Serve Pork slices on a Platter with a little sauce drizzled down the center over the meat

Serve the remaining sauce in a bowl on the side

Red Zinfandel chilled is tasty

Notes:

PULLED-PORK ROAST BEER-STEEPED B.B.Q.

PREPARATION

Pre-heat Oven to 225 degrees

- Score (X) Fat Cap on Pork Butt with carving knife; cut Fat side only and try to cut only the fat
- Place pieces or slices on Jalapeno peppers into cuts made in Fat Cap Coat the entire roast with dry mustard first, then with your dry rub or JERK rub
- Place roast in roasting pan with the FAT side UP and cover with Aluminum foil; put in oven and roast for 2 hours at 225 degrees Remove Aluminum foil and continue to roast for 3 hours at 250 degrees

NOTE: baste or spray roast with Apple juice every 30 minutes After these 3 hours or roasting, remove from oven

- Apply BBQ Marinade to the roast and pour the beer into the roasting pan
- Return roast to Oven and RAISE temp. to 300 degrees
- Cook for additional 5 hours; Spray with apple cider vinegar once an hour and Spray or baste with Apple Juice once an hour - alternate on the half hour

NOTE: after cooking time is up, take temperature of Roast. It should be 170-175 degrees

NOTE: check roast temperature after a total of 8 hours as it might cook quickly; do not cook roast longer than 10 hours total time. Remove roast to a Platter

- Let the roast rest for 5 minutes then, take a fork in each hand and start pulling or shredding the meat.
- You may wish to remove most or all of the Fat before shredding as well as the meat bone. The bone should come apart from the meat easily.
- Once the meat is shredded. spray a little apple cider vinegar or apple juice on the meat

INGREDIENTS

6-8- lb. Boston Butt, Pork Roast, bone-in

I cup of your favorite dry rub or JERK rub

6 cups of your favorite dark beer

1½ cup Apple Cider Vinegar

2 Tablespoons Chili Powder

2 Tablespoons of Cumin, ground

2 Tablespoon of dry mustard

2½ cups dark brown Sugar

2 Tablespoons Red Pepper Flakes, crushed

2 Bay leaves

1 Tablespoon Liquid Smoke

2 tsp cracked Black Pepper

2 tsp Kosher Salt

3 Jalapeno Peppers, pickled in vinegar, rough chopped or sliced thinly on bias

1 Bottle BBQ Sauce (18-22 oz), mild or medium hot

1 can or bottle of dark Molasses; Steen's of Louisiana if possible

RECIPE FOR MARINADE ON NEXT PAGE...

RECIPE FOR MARINADE

In a medium bowl, mix brown sugar, apple cider vinegar, chili powder, Cumin, salt and pepper, red pepper flakes and bay leaves together. Add 113 cup of Dark Molasses (Steen's molasses from Louisiana, if you can get it). Pour over roast during cooking process

PRESENTATION

Serve with Potato Salad and I or Coleslaw and baked beans

Serve on a roll or serve as a plate

Serve with Iced Tea or a Beer

Notes:

BAKED CHICKEN BREAST WITH HONEY-DIJON SAUCE, GOAT CHEESE AND NUTS

INGREDIENTS

4 Chicken Breasts, boneless and skinless

1/4 cup Fresh Honey

1/4 cup Dijon Mustard

1/4 cup of Almond slices or slivers

1/4 cup Walnuts,

1/4 cup Pecans

4 oz. Goat Cheese

1/4 cup Italian Parsley, chopped

Salt and Pepper

PREPARATION

- Mix Dijon mustard and honey together in a bowl and set aside
- Place all the nuts in a food processor or blender and chop until crushed
- PRE-HEAT OVEN to 400 degrees
- Spray baking dish with cooking spray (PAM)
- Place chicken breasts in baking dish and sprinkle with salt and pepper on top and bottom of chicken breasts
- Coat each chicken breast with the Honey-Dijon Sauce
- Sprinkle the crushed nuts over all the chicken breasts
- Put baking dish in Oven at 400 degrees for 30 Minutes, uncovered
- Remove chicken after 30 minutes and crumble goat cheese pieces on each breast
- Add or drizzle some of the Honey- Dijon Sauce over the goat cheese
- Replace in Oven at 350 degrees for 20 minutes
- Remove and sprinkle Parsley over the Chicken Breasts in the baking dish or plate the Chicken and Sprinkle the Parsley over each piece

PRESENTATION

Serve with sour cream mashed potatoes or cooked white rice with frozen peas mixed into the rice

Notes:

TOP HAT PORK CHOPS

THICK-CUT PORK CHOPS IN SILKY CHAMPAGNE AND BLACK OLIVE SAUCE

PREPARATION

IN A LARGE SKILLET:

- Heat the olive oil on high heat
- Season Pork chops with salt and pepper, Thyme and Tarragon
- Place in Hot Skillet with season side down
- Season the remaining side of the Pork Chops
- Cook for TWO minutes and turn the pork chops over
- Cook for another 2 minutes
- Add the Shallots to the pan
- Add the Champagne to the pan
- Cook for another 1 to 2 minutes and remove and reserve the Chops
- Whisk the flour into the milk and add to the pan
- Whisk the sauce in the pan
- Return the pork chops and simmer until the pan sauce thickens
- Remove and place the chops on a large serving platter
- Drain the Black Olives and add them to the sauce for 1 minute
- Drizzle the Sauce over the Pork Chops
- Reserve some sauce to be ladled at the table when plating dinner

INGREDIENTS

4 thick-cut (1 ½ inch) Pork Chops, trimmed of Fat

1/2 cup Shallots, sliced thinly

3 tsp dried Thyme

3 tsp dried Tarragon

Kosher Salt and Cracked Black Pepper to season to taste

1 ½ cup Dry Champagne

1 Tbsp all-purpose Flour

1 cup whole milk or heavy cream (preferred)

2 Tbsp Extra-Virgin Olive Oil

4 oz. Black Olives, sliced

PRESENTATION

Present Pork Chops on a Serving Platter

Drizzle the Sauce over the Pork Chops; Garnish with a Sprig of Parsley

Serve with Carrots and Fennel; Serve with Lemon-Basil New Potatoes

Serve Salade HOLLANDAISE with Lemon Cream Dressing

Above Recipes in my book

Wine: Chilled Red Zinfandel or White Burgundy.

FISH

BAKED SALMON WITH A SOY-GLAZE

PREPARATION

- Place all ingredients in a medium sauce pan under high heat
- Reduce by half or until syrupy consistency
- Remove from the heat and reserve
- Cover a 9" by 13" with aluminum foil
- Spray aluminum foil with cooking spray
- Place 2 (6 oz.) Salmon slices or steaks, skin removed, on the aluminum foil
- Pre-heat oven to 375 degrees
- Brush the top and sides of the salmon with the soy-glaze
- Place the baking sheet with salmon in oven for 20 min.

NOTE: check while cooking to brush with glaze and to test doneness

- Remove and put at rest
- Brush the tops with more glaze and add a sprinkle of sesame seeds
- Garnish with a little pickled ginger (see recipe for pickled ginger)

INGREDIENTS

3 Tbsp Rice Wine Vinegar

3 Tbsp Soy Sauce

2 t Hoisin Sauce

1 Tbsp Dijon Mustard

1 Tbsp Honey

2 t Ginger, peeled and minced

Sesame seeds

PRESENTATION

Serve with a medley of red, yellow bell pepper slices and haricot verte topped with the soy-glaze and sesame seeds

Chilled Chardonnay adds a sparkle

Notes:

ROASTED GINGER SALMON

** Recipe derived from "New New Orleans Cooking" by Emeril Lagasse & Jesse Tirsch Serving Salmon Fillets: Poached or Baked (See Ginger Salmon Recipe)

PREPARATION

- Pre-heat the oven to 400 degrees
- Season Salmon fillets with Emeril's Essence and reserve

IN A SMALL MIXING BOWL COMBINE:

- The Ginger, Orange and Lemon zest and Cilantro. Stir in enough bread crumbs to bind the crust. Add a Tablespoon of fresh squeezed Orange juice if needed to help bind crust. Avoid getting mixture too wet.
- In a sauté pan, heat the oil. When hot, sear the fillets for a minute or two per side (top and bottom)
- Remove from the heat and cover the top side of each fillet with the crust mixture.
- Place in a roasting pan and roast in oven for 8-10 minutes. Crust should be golden in color. Remove from Oven.

PRESENTATION

Spoon or ladle a pool of the sauce into the center of each plate

Place the prepared fillets on the ladled sauce

Drizzle a little sauce over the fillets and around the rim of each plate

OPTIONAL GARNISH:

Sprinkle toasted black and white sesame seeds over the fillets and around the rim of the plate

Place 3 chive stems in any arrangement over each fillet

Wine: Red Zinfandel chilled or your favorite chilled wine

INGREDIENTS

4 Salmon fillets, skin removed, bones removed

1/2 cup fresh grated ginger

2 Tablespoons grated orange zest

2 Tablespoons grated lemon zest

1 cup bread crumbs, Panko plain or seasoned

1/4 cup of Cilantro, fine chopped

Kosher Salt and Cracked black Pepper (a pinch each)

2 Tablespoons of Extra Virgin Olive Oil

6 fried Arugula leaves per serving plate

2 Tablespoon of red peppers, very finely diced (brunoise)

2 Tablespoon of yellow peppers, very finely diced (brunoise)

2 Tablespoon of chopped chives

1 or 2 Tablespoons of Emeril's Original Essence

TUNA STEAKS – MEDITERRANEAN STYLE WITH SOUR CREAM WHIPPED POTATOES

PREPARATION

- Preheat oven to 400 degrees:

IN A LARGE SAUCEPAN:

- Heat 1 tablespoon of Extra Virgin Olive Oil over medium heat.
- Add all peppers, onion, and minced garlic and sauté for 4 minutes.
- Add tomatoes and olives and stir, continue to sauté for 2 minutes.
- Add red wine and water, and stir bringing mixture to a boil.
- Place uncovered in the Oven and cook until thickened and reduced – about 8-10 minutes: stir mixture several times while it is in the oven

ON A LARGE PLATTER:

- Plate the Tuna steaks and rub with 1 tablespoon of Extra Virgin Olive Oil
- Season steaks with salt and pepper mixture
- Sprinkle rosemary needles on the top of each steak
- Reserve steaks, covered with plastic wrap for 15 minutes – do not put in refrigerator
- Heat an ovenproof, non-stick skillet over medium-high heat with remaining tablespoon or two of Extra Virgin Olive Oil until very hot
- Place steaks in hot skillet, rosemary side down
- Sear the steaks for ONE-minute ea.side until slightly browned
- Place seared steaks and skillet in the Oven and bake for 8 to 10 minutes. Do not turn steaks while in the Oven.

SOUR CREAM WHIPPED POTATOES:

- Peel 4 or 5 russet potatoes and quarter them
- Put potatoes in cold water, use pot with a lid; add a pinch of salt
- Bring potatoes to a boil in a covered pot under high heat;

INGREDIENTS

4 Sushi-grade Tuna Steaks, 6oz. Ea.

3 Tbsp, Extra Virgin Olive Oil, use 1 for steak rub

4 cloves of garlic, minced

2 large garden tomatoes, peeled, seeded and chopped

1/4 cup water or stock (chicken or fish) low sodium

12 Kalamata Olives, pitted and sliced

1/4 cup red wine of choice

2 Tbsp fresh rosemary needles, fine-chopped

Kosher salt and cracked black pepper mixed to taste, use for steak rub

3 Tbsp Sour Cream

2 tabs of unsalted butter

2 Tbsp of half and half (milk)

5 russet potatoes, peeled and quartered

12 fresh chive stems for garnish

1 fresh lemon, wedges made for garnish

- Reduce heat, keep pot covered and cook for 15-20 minutes, until fork tender
- Remove potatoes from cook top and drain
- Recover potatoes in pot and reserve for 5 minutes
- Using an electric mixer, whip potatoes, adding sour cream and butter and milk as you mix.
- Add a pinch of salt and pepper, mix again, cover pot and reserve

NOTE:

- Peeling Tomatoes easily:
- Bring a large pot of water to a boil,
- Core the top of the tomatoes and slice a small "X" in the bottom of each tomato with a sharp knife
- Place tomatoes in boiling water for 3 minutes
- Remove and let cool
- Peel and remove seeds
- Chop tomatoes and add to the pepper mixture

PRESENTATION

Place a steak on each plate

Place some of the vegetables on each steak

Place remaining vegetables in a bowl for serving the table

Place wedges of Lemon on left and right side of the steak

Place 3 Chive stems over the vegetables on the steak

Serve Whipped Potatoes either at the side of the steak or as a bed for the steak to diagonally rest on

- Wine: Pinot Noir, chilled or a Fruity white wine

Notes:

SALMON IN A BUNDLE

PREPARATION

- Make a sheet of tin foil for each piece of Salmon; approx. 12 inches long
- In a large mixing bowl, combine the peppers, peas, wine, zest, and lemon juice and Thyme leaves
- Center a handful of the combined product on each piece of Tin Foil
- Place a piece of Salmon on top of each pepper bed; drizzle olive oil over the salmon
- Sprinkle with salt and pepper
- Drizzle the remaining juices over the Salmon pieces
- Place 2 slices of lemon on each Salmon piece
- Close the tin foil to seal in the salmon completely
- Place the "bundles" on a cooking sheet
- Pre-heat oven to 350 degrees
- Place cooking sheet in Oven for 15 min.
- Remove and unwrap the Salmon
- Gingerly, slide the cooked vegetable and Salmon unto your dinner plate

INGREDIENTS

One Red, Yellow, and Green Bell Pepper sliced in strips

1 or 2 cup of Sugar Snap Peas

2 Tbsp Sauvignon wine

2 Tbsp Extra Virgin Olive Oil

Zest of 1 lemon

Juice of 1/2 lemon

2 slices of lemon per piece of Salmon

2 Tbsp dried Thyme leaves

Kosher Salt and Cracked Black Pepper to taste

4 Salmon steaks or straight cuts about 4 oz each piece

PRESENTATION

Serve with a side dish of Rice with golden RAISINS

Serve with a chilled Chardonnay

Notes:

PASTAS

BAKED PASTA AL FORNO

PREPARATION

- Cook the Rigatoni until al dente (about 11 min.)

IN A LARGE FRY PAN:

- Heat olive oil
- Add the sun-dried tomatoes, olives, garlic and eggplant
- Stir and cook until they are softening (about 5 min.)
- Add the tomato puree or crushed tomatoes, stir and cook for 5 additional min.

IN A LARGE MIXING BOWL:

- ADD THE RIGATONI
- ADD THE COOKED VEGETABLES AND MIX

IN A 9" BY 13" BAKING DISH:

- Add 1/2 of the Rigatoni and 1/2 the cooked vegetables
- Add some of the pieces of Mozzarella and Provolone
- Add the remainder of the Rigatoni and vegetables
- Add the remainder of the Mozzarella and Provolone
- TOP the dish with shredded Parmesan
- Bake in a pre-heated oven at 400 degrees for 20 minutes

INGREDIENTS

1 box of Rigatoni

1/2 jar of sun-dried Tomatoes in oil, chopped

1 cup pitted Olives of your choice, sliced lengthwise

3 Tbsp extra virgin olive oil3 garlic cloves, minced

1 eggplant, peeled and sliced and diced or cubed (1 inch size)

I (15 oz.) can of Tomato Puree or crushed tomatoes

1 pkg. of Mozzarella cheese, sliced and diced

1 pkg. Provolone cheese, sliced and diced

1/3 cup Parmesano/ Regiano cheese, grated

PRESENTATION

Make sure the dish is bubbling and browning before you remove it from the oven

Serve immediately with warm and crisp garlic rubbed bread slices

Chianti is the wine of choice for this dish

PASTINA WITH FENNEL, PEAS AND PEPPERS

INGREDIENTS

1 LB. Pasta (Ditalini, Bowtie, or your choice of a small pasta)

1 medium yellow Onion, fine diced

2 carrots, peeled and fine diced or diced in 1/2 inch pieces

1 red and 1 yellow Bell pepper, small diced

1 Fennel Bulb, cored and sliced, then small diced

1 cup low-sodium chicken stock

1 cup frozen Peas, thawed

2 Tbsp Olive Oil or Canola Oil

4 oz. of cream cheese, room temperature

4 oz. of mascarpone cheese, room temperature

A pinch of Kosher salt

3 Tbsp of fresh basil leaves, rolled and chopped

PREPARATION

- Cook the Pasta in boiling, salted water and drain and reserve
- Reserve 1 cup of the Pasta water
- In a large skillet, heat the oil over med. High heat
- Add the Onion and carrots and Fennel; cook until softened (10 min.)
- Add the peppers and the chicken stock; Bring to a boil
- Reduce heat to simmer and cook for 5 minutes
- Add the Peas and the salt, stir and cook for 2 minutes
- Add the cooked Pasta and sir to combine
- Remove from the heat and add the cheeses
- Stir until the mixture is incorporated and the cheeses are melted to form a sauce-like consistency
- Taste and adjust the seasoning as needed
- Remove to a Serving Bowl and garnish with the chopped Basil

PRESENTATION

Serve as a side dish with a Chicken or Pork entrée

Chilled white wine might be welcomed

Notes:

ROTINI IN A HURRY

PREPARATION

- Cook the Pasta until al dente (about 10 min.)
- Using a large Fry Pan:
- Add 2 TBSP of olive oil heat at med. High heat
- Add the garlic and cook for 1 minute
- Add all the Spinach and cook until reduced in volume
- Add the cherry tomatoes and a TBSP of olive oil
- Toss the ingredients and cook for 3 minutes

IN A LARGE MIXING/SERVING BOWL:

- Place the cooked pasta
- Add the cooked vegetables
- Add the grated Asiago cheese and mix the vegetables and the pasta with the cheese
- Add the remaining olive oil and mix
- Add the grated Parmesan cheese and mix and SERVE

INGREDIENTS

1 lb. Rotini or Fusili Pasta noodles

1 lb. Cherry Tomatoes, washed and halved

1 bag of Fresh Baby Spinach Leaves, washed, dried and rough chopped

1/4 cup Extra Virgin Olive Oil

2 Garlic cloves, minced

A pinch of Kosher Salt and cracked black Pepper

1/3 cup grated Asiago cheese

1/2 cup grated Parmesan/regiano cheese

PRESENTATION

Serve when ready and with some toasted pieces of garlic toast

Notes:

ZESTY ROTINI WITH ROMA TOMATOES AND EDAMAME

PREPARATION

- Cook pasta in a large pot of boiling, salted water
- Cook for 8 minutes or until al dente
- Drain the pasta: RESERVE 1 cup of the pasta water
- Place the hot pasta in a large mixing bowl
- Add the tomatoes, olive oil, lemon zest and lemon juice and stir
- Add the salt and pepper and the cheese and 1/2 cup of the pasta water
- Stir to combine all ingredients
- Add the remaining 1/2 cup of pasta water if you need it
- Put the mixed pasta salad in a serving bowl
- Top with chopped parsley and serve

INGREDIENTS

1 lb. frozen, shelled Edamame

6 Roma tomatoes, seeded and diced or 1 pkg of grape tomatoes, sliced

2 lemons, zested

1/4 cup freshly squeezed lemon juice

1/4 cup extra virgin olive oil

1 cup crumbled Feta cheese or crumbled Ricotta salata cheese

1 tsp Kosher Salt

1 tsp cracked black pepper

1 lb. rotini pasta

1/4 cup fresh Italian parsley, chopped

PRESENTATION

Makes a great side dish when served with my recipe: Baked Chicken Thighs with sweet chili sauce

Chianti wine and Tuscan country bread slices. toasted

Notes:

ZITI AND VEGETABLES

PREPARATION

- Cook Pasta in boiling waler until al-dente, then drain and place in a large mixing how
- ADD the cooked Asparagus, Com, Sun-dried Tomatoes and Parsley
- TOSS to coat the Pasta and Vegetables
- ADD the Caesar Dressing to the Bowl and combine with a Spatula
- Sprinkle freshly chopped Basil on top of the Mix and Serve

INGREDIENTS

I lb. cooked Ziti pasta

1 cup cooked asparagus

1 can baby com, drained

1/2 cup sun dried Tomatoes, packed in oil

1/4 cup fresh Italian Parsley. chopped

1/4 cup fresh Basil, chopped

1/2 cup Caesar Dressing or a non-fat Italian dressing

PRESENTATION

Serve with sliced Ciabatta Bread, warmed with a little garlic-butter or rubbed with garlic before warmed

Wine: Chianti of course

Notes:

VEGETABLES

ARTICHOKE GRATIN

INGREDIENTS

3 Tbsp Extra Virgin Olive Oil

2 cloves, garlic, minced

2 pkgs. Frozen Artichoke Hearts, whole or quartered

1/2 cup flat-leaf Parsley

1 pinch, red pepper flakes

1 pinch each of salt and pepper

1/2 cup Chicken Stock

1/2 cup Marsala wine or Madera wine

3 Tbsp unsalted butter, melted

1/3 cup Parmesano/ Regiano cheese, grated

1/3 cup Panko Bread Crumbs

PREPARATION

IN A LARGE FRY PAN:

- Add the olive oil and heat using med. High heat
- Add the minced Garlic, cook for 1 minute
- Add the frozen Artichoke Hearts and stir, continue cooking until softened
- Add the pepper flakes and the parsley, stir to mix
- Add the salt and pepper, wine, Chicken stock and stir

IN A SEPARATE BOWL,

- Combine the melted butter, bread crumbs and cheese
- Mix the ingredients together

IN A 9 BY 13 BAKING DISH:

- Put the artichoke cooked mixture in the dish and smooth it to level
- Pour the buttered bread crumbs and cheese on top to cover the dish
- Add additional cheese if needed to cover the dish
- Put the dish UNCOVERED in the oven at 450 degrees for 10 minutes
- Remove and place the dish in the BROILER on high heat for 3 minutes or until the cheese is bubbly and browning

PRESENTATION

Serve as a side dish with the entrée of your choice. It goes well with Fish and baked Chicken breasts (skinless).

Chardonnay chilled is a good idea.

FIESTA RICE

PREPARATION

- Cook the Rice. When the Rice is half way cooked add the black beans and corn and the salsa. Cook for 10 additional minutes if using regular rice or cook for 3 minutes if using instant.
- Remove from the heat.
- Stir or fluff the rice and add in the Cilantro leaves and stir again
- Season with the Salt and Pepper

INGREDIENTS

1 cup of long-grain Rice, regular or instant

1 can of black beans, drained

1/2 cup of Salsa

1/2 cup of frozen Corn, thawed

3 Tbsp of chopped Cilantro leaves

A pinch of Kosher Salt and Cracked Black Pepper

PRESENTATION

Serve in a Large Bowl

Goes well with Flank Steak or grilled Chicken breasts

Red or White Wine is fine -- but not a sweet wine

Notes:

LEMON-BASIL NEW POTATOES

PREPARATION

- In a large pot put 2 cups of Chicken Broth, low sodium
- Clean and halve the potatoes and add to the pot
- Add 1/2 cup fresh lemon juice
- Add 2 Tbsp of Extra Virgin Olive Oil
- Salt and pepper, a pinch each
- BRING TO A BOIL then turn down to a SIMMER AND COVER THE POT
- Cook until nearly fork tender then DRAIN
- Place potatoes in a large mixing bowl
- Add 2 Tbsp Extra Virgin Olive oil and mix
- Add by sprinkling, the lemon Zest
- Add Salt and pepper to taste
- Chop or chiffenade the Basil leaves and add and gingerly toss

INGREDIENTS

2 LB. New Potatoes

2 cups Chicken Broth, low Sodium

1/2 cup juice from fresh squeezed lemons

4 Tbsp Extra Virgin Olive Oil

A pinch Kosher salt and 5 twists of fresh cracked black pepper

Zest of 1 lemon

8 leaves of fresh Basil, chopped

PRESENTATION

Place potatoes in a large serving bowl

Add a little more zest to the potatoes

Serve with Herb Chicken or Southwest Brisket

Wine: Pinot Grigio or a Cabernet Sauvignon

Notes:

MARINATED BROCCOLI

PREPARATION

- Rinse each stalk of broccoli,
- Cut each large stalk off each within two to three inches of the head
- Split or cut the head into smaller parts. Leave up to 11/2 inches of the smaller or larger stalk.
- Place into large serving bowl.
- Put the next seven ingredients into a small container. Cover and shake vigorously, mixing ingredients thoroughly.
- Pour over broccoli. Toss, coating thoroughly. Marinate from two to twenty-four hours.

INGREDIENTS

3 large stalks Broccoli
1/3-cup salad oil
1/4 cup white vinegar
3 Tbsp light brown sugar
1 Tbsp prepared yellow mustard
1/4 tsp salt (optional)
1/8 tsp pepper
1 clove garlic, chopped finely

PRESENTATION

Looks lovely in a glass serving bowl.

Notes:

ROASTED ASPARAGUS – MEDITERRANEAN STYLE WITH OLIVES AND PEPPERS

PREPARATION

- Preheat Oven to 425 degrees
- Cover a baking sheet with aluminum foil
- Spray covered baking sheet with non-stick cooking spray
- In a large mixing bowl:
- MIX the Shallots, Asparagus, Olives, and Roasted Red Pepper slices
- Drizzle Olive Oil over the vegetables and SPRINKLE with Lemon-Pepper
- TOSS and put the coated vegetables on the covered baking sheet – Spreading them out
- Add a little lemon-pepper if you want and drizzle them with Olive Oil
- Place them in the Oven and cook for 10 minutes or a little longer until the asparagus is a little crispy-tender

INGREDIENTS

1 lb. Asparagus, trimmed and rinsed

1/2 cup Kalamata Olives, pitted, chopped or sliced

2 Tablespoons Extra-Virgin Olive Oil

1 Roasted Red Pepper, julienne sliced

2 Medium Shallots, thin-sliced

2 Tablespoons of Lemon-pepper

PRESENTATION

Serve with Tuna Steak, grilled

Serve with Herb-crusted grilled Chicken Breasts

Serve with Chilled White Wine preferably a Bordeaux

Notes:

SMASHED HOME FRIES

PREPARATION

IN A LARGE POT OF COLD WATER:

- Add the potatoes, whole
- Add 4 garlic cloves, peeled and whole
- Boil the potatoes until done (approx. 15 min.)
- Remove to a large mixing bowl

IN A SKILLET ON HIGH HEAT:

- Melt the butter
- Add 3 tbsp olive oil
- Add the sliced shallots
- Add 2 garlic cloves, chopped or diced
- Cook until softened
- Remove and add to the mixing bowl with the potatoes

IN A LARGE MIXING BOWL:

- Use a potato masher and mashed the potatoes and the shallots and garlic to combine – you can leave the potatoes "lumpy"
- Add the salt and pepper and then using a spoon or a fork, stir the mixture
- Cover the bowl with plastic wrap until ready to use

WHEN READY TO USE:

- Add 2 tbsp olive oil to a skillet on high heat
- Add the potatoes to the skillet
- Add 2 or 3 dashes of hot sauce (Tabasco preferred)
- Mix the potatoes to help make them crispy (3 to 4 minutes)
- Remove and serve

INGREDIENTS

5 medium Yukon gold potatoes, unpeeled

6 cloves of garlic, whole and peeled

1 tbsp Kosher salt

1 tbsp cracked black pepper

2 tbsp unsalted butter

5 tbsp olive oil

3 medium shallots, peeled, thin sliced

Notes:

SANDWICHES

CITY CHICKEN SANDWICH – A LIGHT LUNCH SPECIALTY

CHICKEN, BRIE AND GRANNY SMITH APPLE SANDWICH SERVED OPEN-FACED WITH A DRIZZLE OF BALSAMIC VINEGAR-HONEY DIJON REDUCTION

PREPARATION

- Combine balsamic vinegar and honey and Dijon mustard in a medium sauce pan
- Stir the mixture until combined
- Place on medium-high heat and reduce to half
- Remove and place in a serving bowl
- In a separate fry pan, cook the chicken breasts in a light oil or a canola oil until cooked and slightly browned
- Remove and reserve the chicken when cooked
- Slice the Challah Bread and toast or grill them
- Slice the Brie – 3 slices per serving piece of bread
- Peel the Apple and slice in thin strips

INGREDIENTS

1/2 cup balsamic vinegar

2 Tbsp Dijon Mustard

2 Tbsp Honey

4 slices Challah Bread—slices should be about 1/2 inch thick

13 ounce package of Brie—double creamy style, sliced

2 cooked chicken breasts, skinless and boneless, sliced in thin strips

1 Granny Smith Apple, peeled and sliced in thin strips

THEN ASSEMBLE THE OPEN-FACED SANDWICH AS FOLLOWS

- Place the toast pieces on a serving platter
- Add slices of Brie to each piece (2 or 3 slices per piece)
- Layer Chicken slices on top of Brie
- Drizzle a spoonful of the balsamic reduction over the Chicken pieces
- Layer the apple slices in a thatch weave style on top of the Chicken
- Drizzle some more balsamic reduction over the apple slices

PRESENTATION

Present sandwiches at the table on a serving platter

Place extra balsamic reduction in a serving bowl to use as needed

Serve with a chilled Riesling or a white Zinfandel

Notes:

3-CHEESE CALZONE WITH SUN-DRIED TOMATOES AND BROCCOLI

PREPARATION

- On a large baking sheet:
- Spread some all-purpose flour
- Place the pizza dough on the flour, roll it to smooth it out

IN A LARGE BOWL:

- Mix the Ricotta cheese and the Mozzarella cheese and the thawed Broccoli florets to combine them
- Add the sun-dried tomatoes and combine
- Spoon the cheese and broccoli mixture onto the Pizza dough

NOTE: Put the mixture ONLY ON ONE HALF OF THE DOUGH

- Fold the unused half of the dough over the cheese and broccoli half
- Make sure the ends of the dough come together; use a fork to crimp the edges of the dough to seal them
- Paint a little olive oil over the top of the dough
- Spread the Parmesan cheese liberally over the top of the sealed dough
- Cut several slits in the top of the dough to let steam escape while cooking in the oven
- COOK IN OVEN PRE-HEATED TO 450 DEGREES FOR 12 MINUTES APPROX.

INGREDIENTS

One large piece of Pizza dough (store bought and refrigerated)

One package of frozen Broccoli (1lb)

A container of grated Parmesan cheese

8 oz. of Ricotta cheese

One 16 oz. bag of shredded Mozzarella cheese

1/4 cup sun-dried tomatoes in oil

Optional: 8 oz. of Provolone cheese, shredded

PRESENTATION

Serve when ready – let it cool before slicing

Notes:

BREAKFAST

FRITTATA-FOR BRUNCH WITH SAUSAGE AND PEPPERS

PREPARATION

- PRE-HEAT OVEN TO 350 DEGREES

ON THE STOVE TOP:

- use a non-stick large sauté or fry pan: spray it with olive oil or butter
- Add the crumbled sausage and brown it; add the peppers and sauté until they are soft
- OPTIONAL: add a large shallot, sliced thinly

IN A LARGE MIXING BOWL:

- Beat the eggs, season with a pinch of salt
- Add the Parmesan and stir to combine with the eggs
- Using a rubber, heat-proof spatula, stir the eggs into the pan with the sausage and peppers,
- Stir the eggs to evenly distribute the sausage mixture throughout
- Optional: sprinkle the shallot slices, tomatoes and 1/2 of the Basil leaves over the eggs and sausage mixture

NOTE: once the eggs "set" on the bottom and sides of the fry pan, place the pan in the pre-heated oven and cook for 8 minutes

NOTE: as ovens differ, CHECK to insure doneness before removing the pan

The eggs should be cooked through and the top should be firming and browning

- Remove, let sit for 2-3 minutes

INGREDIENTS

2 Tbsp Extra Virgin Olive Oil

Mix the following sausage types:

Italian, Polish, No. Carolina smoked

Use a 3-inch slice of each type

Remove the skin and crumble the sausage, or cut each slice into 1/2 inch coins

1 red bell pepper, in 1/4 inch dice

1 yellow pepper, in 1/4 inch dice

1 cup freshly grated Parmesan cheese

6 eggs, beaten with 1/4 cup water or milk

A pinch of Kosher Salt

10 Basil leaves, chopped

3 Roma Tomatoes, seeded and quartered, then chopped

PRESENTATION

Cut into wedges and serve hot or at room temperature if preferred

Chilled white wine or a Mimosa.

I prefer a chilled Red Zinfandel and my Anise and Shallot Potato Salad. Recipe found in my first cookbook: 100+ Recipes that Work. It is on page 34

TEXAS TOSTADA A 10-MINUTE BREAKFAST

PREPARATION

- Scramble an egg and add the Sausage crumbles to the scramble
- Add the cheese you like while scrambling
- Add salt and pepper to taste
- Toast or warm an 8-inch Tortilla
- Place the scrambled egg and sausage on the toasted tortilla
- Add the Salsa as a topping
- Add the Parsley as a garnish

INGREDIENTS

(1) 8-inch Tortilla, toasted in a fry pan

1/4 cup Sausage crumbles, prepared in a fry pan

(1) egg scrambled

Add a little Mexican "white" cheese or American "yellow" Cheddar

Add a little Salsa

Add fresh Parsley, chopped as a garnish

Salt and Pepper to taste

PRESENTATION

Serve open-faced and with some sliced Cherry tomatoes

Optional: Add some hash-brown potatoes with red and green bell pepper pieces

Notes:

DESSERTS

BLUEBERRY RICE PUDDING WITH GOLDEN RAISINS AND TOASTED WALNUTS

PREPARATION

- In a medium saucepan stir all ingredients – EXCEPT THE RAISINS AND WALNUTS and bring to a simmer
- Cook the ingredients for 5 minutes and add the cooked rice while stirring frequently until the pudding is thick and creamy
- Add the RAISINS and walnuts and stir
- Remove from the heat
- Place in serving bowls and add some blueberries and cinnamon to each serving

INGREDIENTS

1 cup cooked rice

1 cup whole milk

1/4 cup sugar

3/4 cup Coconut milk

1 tsp ground Cardamom

1 tsp ground cinnamon –plus more for garnish

1/4-1/2 cup DRIED blueberries—plus more for garnish

1/4 cup golden RAISINS and toasted walnuts mixed together

PRESENTATION

Serve warm

Notes:

LIGHT AND LEMONY JELLO CHEESE CAKE

PREPARATION

- Place the can of skimmed evaporated milk in refrigerator for several hours to chill
- Mix the Jell-O with I cup of boiling water and reserve until needed.
- Crush graham crackers with rolling pin or small blender,
- Put crushed crackers into a 9x13 baking dish – reserve 2 tablespoons of crackers.
- Pour melted butter over crackers. Mix in baking dish and press down.
- In a small mixing bowl, mix the cream cheese and sugar. Add the Vanilla and mix
- Using an electric mixer, on low speed add the jello to the cream cheese and vanilla.
- In a large mixing bowl or blender whip the cooled evaporated milk on high speed.
- Mix the cream cheese and jello mixture and add the whipped milk. Blend on medium speed.
- Pour over crust in 9x13 baking dish. Top with extra crust mix. Refrigerate up to six hours before serving.

INGREDIENTS

Crust: 1 ½ cups of graham crackers, crumbled

1 Stick butter, room temperature

Cake Mix:

1 small package lemon Jell-O

1 eight oz. package Philadelphia cream cheese

1 cup granulated sugar

2 tsp vanilla

1 can skimmed evaporated milk

PRESENTATION

Garnish your cake with a few thin slices of curled lemon wedges or dot the surface with blueberries or sliced strawberries

Notes:

TIRAMISU WITH A VERY BERRY TWIST

PREPARATION

- In a large mixing bowl:
- Using an electric mixer, BEAT the whipping cream until thickened
- While beating, slowly add the sugar, beating until soft peaks form
- Gradually, stir in the softened cheese until combined; when done, set aside
- In a 9" x 13" baking dish:
- Split the ladyfingers and place them cut side up to line the bottom of the dish
- Brush ladyfingers with the limeade concentrate
- Spoon half of the cheese mixture over the ladyfingers and smooth it across all of them
- Top the layer with half of the blueberry pie filling
- REPEAT the process for the next layer with the ladyfingers, limeade, cheese mixture and pie filling.
- Cover the dish and chill for 8 hours.
- Note: Garnish with chopped fresh mint if desired

INGREDIENTS

1 Pint of Heavy Whipping Cream

1/4 cup powdered sugar (confectioner's)

1 lb. Mascarpone cheese, softened to warm temperature

3 packages of unfilled ladyfingers

1 (60z.) can frozen limeade concentrate or raspberry concentrate, thawed

1 (21-oz.) can blueberry pie filling

Fresh mint leaves, optional

PRESENTATION

Serve with a chilled Riesling and slice at the table setting

Notes:

CPSIA information can be obtained at www.ICGtesting.com
Printed in the USA
LVOW131947070212

267599LV00001B/1/P

9 780982 943748